THE FUTURE OF DEMOCRACY AND GOVERNANCE IN LIBERIA

HEARING

BEFORE THE

SUBCOMMITTEE ON AFRICA, GLOBAL HEALTH, GLOBAL HUMAN RIGHTS, AND INTERNATIONAL ORGANIZATIONS

OF THE

COMMITTEE ON FOREIGN AFFAIRS
HOUSE OF REPRESENTATIVES

ONE HUNDRED FIFTEENTH CONGRESS

FIRST SESSION

SEPTEMBER 13, 2017

Serial No. 115–63

Printed for the use of the Committee on Foreign Affairs

Available via the World Wide Web: http://www.foreignaffairs.house.gov/ or
http://www.gpo.gov/fdsys/

U.S. GOVERNMENT PUBLISHING OFFICE

26–837PDF   WASHINGTON : 2017

COMMITTEE ON FOREIGN AFFAIRS

EDWARD R. ROYCE, California, *Chairman*

CHRISTOPHER H. SMITH, New Jersey
ILEANA ROS-LEHTINEN, Florida
DANA ROHRABACHER, California
STEVE CHABOT, Ohio
JOE WILSON, South Carolina
MICHAEL T. McCAUL, Texas
TED POE, Texas
DARRELL E. ISSA, California
TOM MARINO, Pennsylvania
JEFF DUNCAN, South Carolina
MO BROOKS, Alabama
PAUL COOK, California
SCOTT PERRY, Pennsylvania
RON DeSANTIS, Florida
MARK MEADOWS, North Carolina
TED S. YOHO, Florida
ADAM KINZINGER, Illinois
LEE M. ZELDIN, New York
DANIEL M. DONOVAN, JR., New York
F. JAMES SENSENBRENNER, JR.,
  Wisconsin
ANN WAGNER, Missouri
BRIAN J. MAST, Florida
FRANCIS ROONEY, Florida
BRIAN K. FITZPATRICK, Pennsylvania
THOMAS A. GARRETT, JR., Virginia

ELIOT L. ENGEL, New York
BRAD SHERMAN, California
GREGORY W. MEEKS, New York
ALBIO SIRES, New Jersey
GERALD E. CONNOLLY, Virginia
THEODORE E. DEUTCH, Florida
KAREN BASS, California
WILLIAM R. KEATING, Massachusetts
DAVID N. CICILLINE, Rhode Island
AMI BERA, California
LOIS FRANKEL, Florida
TULSI GABBARD, Hawaii
JOAQUIN CASTRO, Texas
ROBIN L. KELLY, Illinois
BRENDAN F. BOYLE, Pennsylvania
DINA TITUS, Nevada
NORMA J. TORRES, California
BRADLEY SCOTT SCHNEIDER, Illinois
THOMAS R. SUOZZI, New York
ADRIANO ESPAILLAT, New York
TED LIEU, California

AMY PORTER, *Chief of Staff*   THOMAS SHEEHY, *Staff Director*
JASON STEINBAUM, *Democratic Staff Director*

———

SUBCOMMITTEE ON AFRICA, GLOBAL HEALTH, GLOBAL HUMAN RIGHTS, AND
INTERNATIONAL ORGANIZATIONS

CHRISTOPHER H. SMITH, New Jersey, *Chairman*

MARK MEADOWS, North Carolina
DANIEL M. DONOVAN, JR., New York
F. JAMES SENSENBRENNER, JR.,
  Wisconsin
THOMAS A. GARRETT, JR., Virginia

KAREN BASS, California
AMI BERA, California
JOAQUIN CASTRO, Texas
THOMAS R. SUOZZI, New York

C O N T E N T S

Page

WITNESSES

LETTERS, STATEMENTS, ETC., SUBMITTED FOR THE HEARING

APPENDIX

THE FUTURE OF DEMOCRACY AND GOVERNANCE IN LIBERIA

WEDNESDAY, SEPTEMBER 13, 2017

House of Representatives,
Subcommittee on Africa, Global Health,
Global Human Rights, and International Organizations,
Committee on Foreign Affairs,
Washington, DC.

The subcommittee met, pursuant to notice, at 2:00 p.m., in room 2172 Rayburn House Office Building, Hon. Christopher H. Smith (chairman of the subcommittee) presiding.

Mr. SMITH. The subcommittee will come to order, and good afternoon to everyone.

On the eve of the Liberian election, I want especially thank Congressman Dan Donovan for recommending this important hearing for our subcommittee before those elections and also to speak to the future of democracy and governance in Liberia.

As we all know, of the more than 50 nations in Africa, the United States has the closest connection with the Republic of Liberia.

This is not only because Liberia was founded in 1847 by freed men and former slaves from this country, but also because of the estimated 500,000 Liberians and Liberian descendants who live here.

Liberian cities such as Monrovia and Buchanan were named for American Presidents and—in part of my district that I had for 30 years before it was redistricted out—the city of Trenton has a very large Liberian diaspora population with whom I got very close, and still do a great deal of case work for even though I don't represent them because that bond is so strong.

However, most Americans are largely unaware of the long link between United States and Liberia and likely see Liberia as just another African country.

Most Americans are unaware that Liberia has been a major U.S. ally since World War II and into the Cold War, hosting U.S. communications facilities in the 1960s and 1970s, and has received extensive U.S. development assistance including post-war aid and Ebola aid to Liberia.

The United States has also helped Liberia build its criminal justice sector and supported transitional justice efforts.

U.S. has funded just over a quarter of the cost of United Nations Mission in Liberia (UNMIL) at a cost of about $106 million annually as of fiscal year 2016.

Liberia is also implementing a $256.7 million 5-year MCC compact signed in 2015 designed to increase access to reliable affordable electricity and enhance the country's poor road infrastructure. Bilateral State Department and United States AGency for International Development (USAID) assistance totaled $91 million in Fiscal Year 2016. President Ellen Johnson Sirleaf has made some advancement in democracy and governing during her two terms, and we applaud her for that, following the despotic rule of Charles Taylor.

During his term of office, Taylor was accused of war crimes and crimes against humanity as a result of his involvement in the Sierra Leone civil war from 1991 to 2002. He was also responsible for serious human rights violations in Liberia as well.

Charles Taylor was formally indicted by the Special Court for Sierra Leone in 2003, and I would note parenthetically that the chief prosecutor has been before this subcommittee, David Crane, many times and has provided useful insights as to what we need to do with regards to Syria and war crimes tribunals in another part of the world, all of that information, all of that wisdom gleaned from his work on the Special Court, which not only indicted but prosecuted successfully many, and eventually Charles Taylor, who as we all know, got 50 years and is currently serving that sentence at The Hague.

The United States occasionally arrested the alleged perpetrators of civil rights human rights abuses, often using the immigration perjury charges as a vehicle for prosecution. One of them was Charles McArther Emmanuel, also known as Chuckie Taylor, the son of Charles Taylor.

Raised in Florida, Emmanuel became the commander of the infamously violent Anti-Terrorist Unit, commonly known in Liberia as the Demon Forces.

He is currently serving a 97-year sentence back in Florida for his role in human rights violations carried out by that so-called Anti-Terrorist Unit.

President Sirleaf was unable to, under the constitution, run for a third term. But unlike many other leaders around the world, including in Africa, she did not push to change the constitution to allow a third term.

We don't know yet whether her successors can and will continue her upward trend. Most candidates for President have highlighted corruption.

But as our witnesses from the National Democratic Institute (NDI) can tell us, these candidates have platforms that are light on policy specifics.

Consequently, today's hearing is intended to examine the prospects for democracy and governance in Liberia following the October elections which we hope will be free and fair and transparent. The United States is a key provider of technical assistance to Liberia's national election commission including the International Foundation for Electoral Systems program funded by USAID and the U.N. Development Programme backed by nearly $12 million in mostly European Union funding under a multi-faceted project from 2015 to 2018.

The election commission also receives broader institutional capacity building support under a second $4 million USAID-funded program, the Liberian Administrative and Systems Strengthening. Our Government has a significant investment in Liberia on several fronts. The future direction of this important country is important to the United States.

Therefore, we have a stake in the next government, building on the advances made in democracy and governance, again, under President Johnson Sirleaf.

Most of all, there must be much more done to minimize the impact of corruption in Liberia. It is a serious issue and hopefully our Government, working in tandem with a new government, will really do a major effort along those lines.

I would like to yield to our distinguished ranking member, Ms. Bass.

Ms. BASS. Thank you very much, Mr. Chair, and especially for this timely hearing, considering that we are a few weeks away from an election in Liberia.

So on October 10th we know that Liberians will select a new President, Vice President, and Members of their House. The upcoming elections mark an important moment for the country because they are expected to lead to the country's first electoral transfer of power.

And before we delve into democracy, governance, and the future of Liberia, I actually wanted to take a moment to highlight Madam Ellen Johnson Sirleaf as she ends her second term in presidency. It was such an international event when she became the first female President on the continent of Africa. In 2005, she was charged with the seemingly insurmountable challenge of building a country impacted by 14 years of civil war where more than 200,000 people were killed.

Most of the national infrastructure was destroyed and the country was burdened by enormous debt. I remember when President Johnson Sirleaf came to the United States and to the House many times when Power Africa was established because, if you remember, Liberia was not included in the Power Africa proposal, and she walked the halls of Congress until that was changed and Liberia was included.

During her 12 years of the presidency, a decade of sanctions was lifted and deemed no longer necessary. The economy has drastically improved and averaged more than 7 percent annual growth.

Per capita income has risen from a low point of just $80 at the end of the second civil war in 2003 to $700 even though the population has increased by nearly 50 percent to just under 5 million and life expectancy is up from 53 to 61 years.

And I think that is particularly remarkable, given the setback that the Ebola crisis presented, and the Ebola crisis was certainly an example of what happens when the health infrastructure deteriorates how that was—that disease spread so quickly but yet the country rebounded in spite of it.

We know that the country has also made great progress in rebuilding its infrastructure and its democratic institutions. And finally, President Sirleaf has been a strong proponent of equal rights for women and a champion for youth.

We all applaud and acknowledge her hard work which has also been recognized by the international community, most notably when she was awarded the Nobel Peace Prize.

I also want to point out—I was in Ghana in January for the inauguration of the President, and President Sirleaf there as the head of Economic Community of West African States (ECOWAS) and to see the leadership that she took as the head of ECOWAS in resolving the conflict in the Gambia, which certainly could have deteriorated in a terrible way.

Returning to the topic of this hearing, which is the future of democracy and governance in Liberia, I want to highlight that another extremely important and final act that the President will take is to adhere to Liberia's constitution and step aside in order to allow the democratic process to continue as the people of Liberia choose their next President.

I am happy to say also that President Johnson Sirleaf will be here next Friday as part of the annual legislative conference of the Congressional Black Caucus Foundation and we look forward to her remarks that she will make in a presentation a week from Friday in the morning.

I was honored to be a part of NDI's delegation to Kenya to observe the election. I am sorry I won't be able to participate this time in October.

I look forward to hearing from the representative from the National Endowment for Democracy (NED), who I am sure will talk about the upcoming observations.

I am also glad to see that we have an acting Assistant Secretary—we have all been worried about that for a while—and an acting Assistant Administrator to USAID. So I look forward to your comments.

Thank you.

Mr. SMITH. Thank you very much, Ms. Bass.

I would like to yield to Congressman Dan Donovan.

Mr. DONOVAN. Chairman, I am going to yield my time for when I chair the second panel. I will do my opening statement. Thank you, sir.

Mr. SMITH. Thank you.

I would like to welcome our two distinguished witnesses and, certainly, Donald Yamamoto is no stranger to this subcommittee and to the work that he will be speaking to and I want to thank him for his leadership.

He is the acting Assistant Secretary to Bureau of African Affairs at State. He also served as Principal Deputy Assistant Secretary of State in the Bureau of African Affairs from 2003 to 2006 where he was responsible for coordinating U.S. policy toward more than 20 countries in East and Central Africa.

He served as our Ambassador to Ethiopia from 2006 to 2009 and also the U.S. Ambassador to the Republic of Djibouti from 2000 to 2003 and was the Deputy Director for East African Affairs from 1998 to 2000 and he has, again, testified several times before this committee and, again, we thank him for his service.

Then Cheryl Anderson who is the acting Assistant Administrator for the Bureau of Africa at the U.S. Agency for International Development.

Ms. Anderson has more than 20 years of development experience, mostly in Africa. Before joining USAID as a Foreign Service Officer, she worked in USAID missions in the Democratic Republic of Congo, Uganda, Sudan, and East Africa.

Prior to joining USAID, she worked as a program manager for Healthlink Worldwide and also served as a Peace Corps volunteer in Ghana.

Mr. Secretary, if you could begin.

STATEMENT OF THE HONORABLE DONALD YAMAMOTO, ACTING ASSISTANT SECRETARY, BUREAU OF AFRICAN AFFAIRS, U.S. DEPARTMENT OF STATE

Mr. YAMAMOTO. Thank you very much.

I would like to submit the longer statement for the record.

Mr. SMITH. Without objection, so ordered.

Mr. YAMAMOTO. Representative Smith, thank you very much. Congresswoman Bass and Congressman Donovan, thank you very much. It is a great honor to be back here today.

Good afternoon. Although the 2014-15 Ebola epidemic had a massive human impact and slowed economic growth worldwide, the response led by the United States helped Liberia overcome Ebola and return the country to the path of building confidence.

It is hard to overstate the enormity of the challenge President Ellen Johnson Sirleaf inherited in 2005. We applaud the respect she had demonstrated for Liberia's constitution throughout her tenure and the positive example she has set for the continent of Africa by her unbending respect for Presidential term limits.

Next month, Liberia's citizens will go the polls to facilitate Liberia's first peaceful transition of power between democratically-elected leaders since 1944.

Despite how far Liberia has come, many challenges remain that will fall to President Sirleaf's successor to address. On the elections and security, the Presidential candidates vying to replace President Sirleaf have been campaigning vigorously since the start of the formal campaign period at the end of July.

We are pleased that 20 registered political parties declared their commitment to a peaceful electoral process and many of them reaffirmed this commitment on the margins of the ECOWAS summit in June 2017.

While the United States does not support any specific party or candidate, we are pleased to see a robust participation in this election.

Liberians from all walks of life are aware of the importance of these elections and the United States stands by those committed to support a peaceful, credible, and transparent electoral process.

Despite very real challenges, President Sirleaf and her administration are committed to conducting a peaceful, credible, and transparent election.

The government has also taken steps to build systems and processes led by the Governance Commission for the handover of power that will occur in January 2018.

There are significant challenges still facing the National Electoral Commission notably: Poor infrastructure, inadequate funding, heavy rain that could complicate election logistics.

However, we are encouraged that the NEC successfully carried out a free and fair legislative bi-election this past February.

We are providing comprehensive program support to the Liberian National Election Commission, civil society organizations, media outlets in the run-up to the 2017 elections.

In addition, our Ambassador is meeting with candidates running for President to emphasize the importance of peaceful elections and transitioning government that builds upon the progress made in the last 12 years.

As UNMIL looks to close out its mandate at the end of March 2018, it should be considered a success story. It has kept the peace and gradually but steadily transferred key responsibilities back to government.

The U.N. Mission to Liberia presently is mandated, notably, to protect civilians, advise the Liberian National Police on election security, and promote sustainable peace through its radio station.

Since July 2016, the Government of Liberia has been fully responsible for the internal security and we have seen no discernible change in this society's situation since then.

A joint security task force chaired by the Liberian National Police is also actively overseeing the election security planning. This is a positive sign for prospects of maintaining peace and stability during the electoral period.

On governance, the next President of Liberia will inherit a more stable and secure Liberia than that which President Sirleaf inherited in 2005.

While some drivers of instability have diminished, others will need continued attention. These include deficiencies in the administration of justice, official corruption, land disputes, intertribal, interethnic, and interreligious tensions, poverty coupled with income disparity, and a large youth populations disproportionately affected by unemployment.

Liberia has come a long way in rebuilding state institutions after years of conflict. Nevertheless, the gains are fragile and there is still room for much improvement.

Official and systemic corruption drains limited public resources, deters investment and contributes to a culture in which working in government can be perceived more as a route to self-enrichment than public service.

There is continued need to strengthen institutions critical to democratic governance to ensure improvements are sustained.

As we look ahead, I can assure you the United States remains steadfast in its support for the people of Liberia in their efforts to consolidate further democratic gains, ensure their government remains accountable to its citizens, reduce corruption, ensure the responsible stewardship of scarce public resources.

And with that, I welcome your questions.

[The prepared statement of Mr. Yamamoto follows:]

FINAL- AF

**Statement by Acting Assistant Secretary Donald Yamamoto
"The Future of Democracy and Governance in Liberia"
House Foreign Affairs Committee
Subcommittee on Africa, Global Health, Global Human Rights, and
International Organizations**

September 13, 2017

Good afternoon, and thank you, Mr. Chairman, and members of the Committee, for the opportunity to testify. The United States and Liberia share a special bond that dates to the first days of Liberia's republic, and today that bond is stronger than ever.

Since the end of the Liberian civil war in 2003, the country has improved security for its people, held three free and fair national elections, and taken on the difficult tasks of rebuilding its economy and strengthening its education and health care systems. Although the 2014-2015 Ebola epidemic had a massive human impact and slowed economic growth, a worldwide response led by the United States helped Liberia overcome Ebola and return the country to the path of building confidence.

It is hard to overstate the enormity of the challenge President Ellen Johnson Sirleaf inherited in 2005. We applaud the respect she has demonstrated for Liberia's constitution throughout her tenure, and the positive example she has set for the continent of Africa in her unbending respect for Presidential term limits.

Next month, Liberia's citizens will go to the polls to facilitate Liberia's first peaceful transition of power between democratically-elected leaders since 1944. This election is critical, not just for what the transition represents but because it will give Liberians the opportunity to elect a President well-equipped to lead the country towards a peaceful and prosperous future. Despite how far Liberia has come, many challenges remain that will fall to President Sirleaf's successor to address.

This afternoon, I would like to discuss Liberia's election process, its political transition, and some areas for sustained attention moving forward. While it is not the role of the United States to predict a winner, three things are clear: the Liberian Government is committed to and prepared for a smooth transition of power, the next President of Liberia will continue to contend with governance challenges, and the United States will remain committed to working with the new administration in Liberia to overcome these challenges.

Elections and Security

The presidential candidates vying to replace Sirleaf have been campaigning vigorously since the start of the formal campaign period at the end of July. We are pleased that 20 registered political parties declared their commitment to a peaceful electoral process, and many of them reaffirmed this commitment on the margins of the ECOWAS Summit in June 2017.

While the United States does not support any specific party or candidate, we are pleased to see robust participation in this election. Liberians from all walks of life are aware of the importance of these elections and the United States stands by those committed to supporting a peaceful, credible, and transparent electoral process.

Despite very real challenges, President Sirleaf and her administration are committed to conducting a peaceful, credible, and transparent election. The government has also taken steps to build systems and processes, led by a Governance Commission, for the handover of power that will occur in January 2018.

There are significant challenges still facing the National Elections Commission (NEC), notably poor infrastructure, inadequate funding, and heavy rain that could complicate election logistics. However, we are encouraged that the NEC successfully carried out a free and fair legislative by-election this past February.

We are providing comprehensive programming support to the Liberian National Elections Commission (NEC), civil society organizations, and media outlets in the run-up to the 2017 elections. In addition, our Ambassador is meeting with candidates running for president to emphasize the importance of peaceful elections, and a transition in government that builds upon the progress made in the last 12 years.

As UNMIL looks to close out its mandate at the end of March 2018, it should be considered a success story. It has kept the peace, and gradually but steadily transferred key responsibilities back to the government. The UN Mission in Liberia presently is mandated notably to protect civilians, advise the Liberian National Police on elections security, and promote sustainable peace through its radio station.

Since July 2016, the Government of Liberia has been fully responsible for internal security, and we have seen no discernable change in the security situation since then. A Joint Security Task Force, chaired by the Liberian National Police, is also actively overseeing election security planning. This is a positive sign for prospects of maintaining peace and stability during and after the election period.

Governance

The next President of Liberia will inherit a more stable and secure Liberia than that which President Sirleaf inherited in 2005. While some drivers of instability have diminished, others will need continued attention. These include deficiencies in the administration of justice; official corruption; land disputes; inter-tribal, inter-ethnic, and inter-religious tensions, poverty coupled with income disparity; and a large youth population disproportionately affected by unemployment.

Liberia has come a long way in rebuilding state institutions after years of conflict. Nevertheless, the gains are fragile and there is still room for much improvement. Official and systemic corruption drains limited public resources, deters foreign investment, and contributes to a culture in which working in government can be perceived more as a route to self-enrichment than public service. There is a continued need to strengthen institutions critical to democratic governance to ensure improvements are sustained.

As we look ahead, I can assure you the United States remains steadfast in its support for the people of Liberia in their efforts to consolidate further democratic gains, ensure their government remains accountable to its citizens, reduce corruption, and ensure the responsible stewardship of scarce public resources. We will also continue to work with other donors to make available more affordable, reliable power to the people of Liberia, which is key to Liberia's post-Ebola recovery.

Conclusion

In conclusion, the Government of Liberia has signaled its commitment to a free, fair, and transparent election in October, with a possible second round in November; and to an historic, peaceful, democratic transition of power.

Notwithstanding logistical challenges in completing the electoral process and even greater challenges facing the victors, we look to Liberia's election as another positive step forward for democracy in West Africa.

I would like to thank you, Mr. Chairman, and members of the Committee for your continued interest, and for all the efforts and support that you have dedicated to Liberia and the region. As its largest bilateral partner, the United States will continue to be instrumental in helping the new Government of Liberia move forward.

I welcome your questions on my testimony or any others you might have for me at this time.

———

Mr. SMITH. Thank you very much, Mr. Ambassador.

Ms. Anderson.

STATEMENT OF MS. CHERYL ANDERSON, ACTING ASSISTANT ADMINISTRATOR, BUREAU FOR AFRICA, U.S. AGENCY FOR INTERNATIONAL DEVELOPMENT

Ms. ANDERSON. Good afternoon, Chairman Smith, Ranking Member Bass, Congressman Donovan.

Thank you for inviting me to speak today. I appreciate your considered interest in how U.S. policies and assistance programs can help Liberians consolidate a peaceful and stable democracy in which prosperity is available to all.

USAID's development partnership with Liberia dates back to our founding in 1961. As the largest bilateral donor in Liberia, today the United States plays an influential role in many aspects of the country's development.

Our programs address the underlying structural and institutional problems that gave rise to 14 years of civil strife and war while at the same time tackling the country's more immediate development needs and challenges.

As the new government is formed following the upcoming election, the United States will build strategically on the current strong relationship.

We will identify opportunities to enhance transparency, strengthen checks and balances and support Liberians both inside and outside of government institutions.

This includes our work with the nation's next generation of democratic leaders. If successful, this election will result in the country's first peaceful democratically elected transition of power in more than 70 years, marking a critical milestone in the country's progress toward a stable democracy.

Recent USAID assessments indicate that citizens are excited about the election and remain actively engaged in the political process.

While the campaign period had proceeded smoothly to date with political parties and candidates conducting themselves peacefully, the National Elections Commission is still fairly limited in its capacity.

There may by logistical challenges exacerbated by the limited infrastructure across the country, especially given the timing of the elections during the rainy season.

USAID continues to support elections preparations including support to address necessary preparation that is facing the National Elections Commission.

This support has three core pillars. The first improves the performance, transparency, and accountability of the commission, which, in turn, builds public confidence in the elections.

Second, we support citizen participation in electoral processes as voters, as activists, and as candidates, and third, we strengthen civil society and media monitoring of the electoral process.

USAID has partnered with local media and civil society organizations including youth, women, and trade unions to educate first-time and hard-to-reach voters about the stakes in the 2017 elections, and encourage their peaceful participation.

Also, we continue to build the communication capacity of the Elections Commission. This includes support for regular meetings between the commission and political parties to share information and to help resolve electoral issues before they escalate.

USAID supported domestic and international observation missions, continued to provide reports on the pre-electoral process.

The Sirleaf administration remains publicly committed to conducting a free, fair, and transparent election in October and to an orderly transition of power to the incoming administration. USAID remains committed to partnering with Liberia during that transition.

I would be remiss if I did not acknowledge and thank you for the critical support provided by Congress through the United States emergency assistance to Liberia during and after the Ebola epidemic.

With donor support, the government was able to control the epidemic, which many predicted would have been far worse. We must continue to invest in strengthening institutions to further improve public administration and communication functions at national and local levels and to enable citizens to hold their government accountable.

This will enable the government to respond to potential future emergencies and ensure the cooperation of the public in adhering to public health guidance.

In summary, we believe that the Government of Liberia can create conditions for a credible electoral process from the pre-election period through the transparent tabulation and announcement of results.

USAID will continue to support these efforts. We will urge the newly-elected administration to consolidate democratic gains through effective and accountable governance that is responsive to the citizens and to adhere to the rule of law.

This includes developing and utilizing systems that reduce opportunities for corruption and waste of limited public resources.

Thank you, Mr. Chairman, Ranking Member Bass, and members of the subcommittee for the continued commitment you have shown to the Liberian people.

I welcome any questions you might have.

[The prepared statement of Ms. Anderson follows:]

Testimony of U.S. Agency for International Development
Acting Assistant Administrator for Africa, Cheryl L. Anderson
before the House Subcommittee on Africa, Global Health, Global Human Rights, and
International Organizations

September 13, 2017
"The Future of Democracy and Governance in Liberia"

INTRODUCTION

Good afternoon Chairman Smith, Ranking Member Bass, and members of the Subcommittee. Thank you for inviting me to speak today. I appreciate your continued interest in how U.S. policies and assistance programs can help Liberians consolidate a peaceful and stable democracy in which prosperity is available to all.

BACKGROUND

USAID's development partnership with Liberia dates back to our founding in 1961. As the largest bilateral donor in Liberia, the United States plays an influential role in many aspects of the country's development. We support the Government of Liberia's development vision as articulated in its 2013 Agenda for Transformation. Our programs in Liberia address the underlying structural and institutional problems that gave rise to fourteen years of civil strife and war, while at the same time tackling the country's more immediate development needs, including power or health challenges, often in close coordination with other U.S. Government agencies such as Millennium Challenge Corporation or the Centers for Disease Control and Prevention.

Since the end of the Liberian civil war in 2003, the country has made notable progress in a number of areas. This includes the nurturing of a vibrant media and active civil society; civil service and public financial management reforms; and the rehabilitation of infrastructure. Despite these important gains, the country continues to face numerous development and economic growth challenges, as Liberia's human development index indicators remains among the lowest in the world. Public institutions remain weak and are often corrupt, contributing to a sense that civil and political rights have not led to more effective governance or economic gains. The Ebola crisis revealed fundamental weaknesses in the citizen-state relationship, undercutting citizen confidence that the government can protect the public and provide services. These and other conditions drive USAID's involvement in Liberia.

It is in the interest of the United States to build upon the progress that has been made and maintain our commitment to help the Liberian people avert crises and live healthier lives. The United States has dedicated significant resources for over a decade to help the country remain on a path of democratic governance and stability. Emerging in late 2003 from two decades of civil conflict, Liberia's recovery presented opportunities for peaceful development, rather than destabilization, in West Africa. Our assistance first focused on reintegration and revitalization activities that gave citizens and communities hope, and led the way to successful elections in 2005 and 2011. Post-conflict countries are most at risk of backsliding during the five-to-ten years following its first elections, so recent USAID activities have focused on strengthening the rule of law, while also building capacity within government and in the education, health and economic sectors to deliver services.

A notable highlight of this effort has been our ongoing support to improved governance and management of the economy, which has been successful in helping the Liberian government control its public finances. As a new government is formed following the upcoming elections, the United States will look to build strategically on the current strong relationship and identify opportunities to enhance transparency, strengthen checks and balances, and to support Liberians both inside and outside of government institutions. This includes our work with the nation's next generation of democratic leaders.

2017 PRESIDENTIAL ELECTIONS
Next month's historic presidential elections present a vital cross road that should reaffirm Liberia's democratic gains and political stability. President Ellen Johnson-Sirleaf will step down at the end of her term, ushering in a newly elected government after 12 years of rule. If successful, this election will result in the country's first peaceful democratic transition in more than 70 years, marking a critical milestone in the country's progress toward a stable democracy. With a peaceful transition in 2018, Liberia will serve as a strong democratic role model for other countries emerging from conflict. At this point in time, there is no clear frontrunner in the presidential race, and it continues to be a highly competitive process.

Recent USAID assessments indicate that citizens are excited about the election and remain actively engaged in the political process. While the campaign period has proceeded smoothly to date, with political parties and candidates conducting themselves peacefully, the National Elections Commission is still fairly limited in its capacity, and there may be logistical challenges exacerbated by limited infrastructure across the country given the timing of the elections during the rainy season. This will be the first election carried out without significant support from the United Nations Mission in Liberia, which ended its security presence in 2016. USAID continues to support elections preparations, including support to address challenges facing the National Elections Commission. This support has three core pillars: our work first builds public confidence in the elections by improving the performance, transparency, and accountability of the Commission; second, we support citizen participation in electoral processes as voters, activists, and candidates; and third we strengthen civil society and media oversight of the electoral process.

USAID has partnered with local media and civil society organizations, including youth, women and trade unions, to educate first-time and hard-to-reach voters about the stakes in the 2017 elections and encourage their peaceful participation. In parallel, we continue to build the communication capacity of the electoral commission. This includes support for regular meetings between the Commission and political parties to share information and help resolve electoral issues before they escalate. USAID-supported domestic and international observation missions continue to receive accreditation from the Commission and are reporting on the pre-electoral process.

The Sirleaf administration remains publicly committed to conducting a free, fair, and transparent election in October and an orderly transition of power to the incoming elected administration, and USAID remains committed to partnering with Liberia during that transition.

USAID SUPPORT

At this critical juncture, we must simultaneously redouble efforts to tackle the significant challenges that remain, while acknowledging the progress Liberia has made in 14 years of peace. Rent-seeking behavior and corruption in Liberia are one of the largest constraints to good governance and are pervasive throughout government. Critical checks, balances, and accountability systems either do not exist or are ineffective, which undermines public trust in state institutions. The formal justice system, a key accountability mechanism for democratic governance, struggles to administer justice due to low capacity. The Liberia Anti-Corruption Commission was created in 2008, but has been hampered by resource, capacity, and political challenges, and its work has resulted in few convictions.

However, we have seen progress in the Government of Liberia's public financial management systems. Today, there is more standardized, transparent reporting and monitoring of financial resources. Fiscal reports for central government and state-owned enterprises are more visible and accessible than at any time in the country's history. County Service Centers that deliver critical government services to the people are operational in ten counties, with openings planned in the remaining five counties in the coming months. Simultaneously, with USAID support, the Government of Liberia is undertaking reforms to generate more local revenue by improving tax policy and collection.

With critical donor support, the Government of Liberia has strengthened its budgeting and fiscal management; improved pay, performance, and payroll management of civil servants; and has strengthened the capacity of both government actors and civil society to reduce corruption. They have also taken steps to decentralize government services to make sub-national resource management more effective and accountable.

Moving forward, Liberia must continue to strengthen institutions critical to the foundations for democratic governance and to prioritize key reforms that deepen the accountability of government systems and processes. Moreover, if Liberian institutions, citizens, donors and partners focus our collective efforts, we can help end the pervasive corruption that threatens to undermine democratic progress, weaken citizen trust in state institutions, and hamper overall development across the country.

I would be remiss if I did not acknowledge and thank you for the critical support provided by Congress, through the United States emergency assistance to Liberia during and after the Ebola epidemic. With donors' support, the Government was able to control the epidemic, which many predicted would have been far worse. We must continue to invest in strengthening institutions to further improve public administration and communication functions at national and local levels and continue to enable citizens to hold their government accountable. This will enable the government to respond to potential future emergencies and ensure the cooperation of the public in adhering to public health guidance.

CONCLUSION

In summary, USAID would like to emphasize our long-standing relationship with the Liberian people and highlight our commitment to accompany Liberia through this historic transition. We believe that the Government of Liberia can create conditions for a credible electoral process, from the pre-election period through the transparent tabulation and announcement of results, and USAID will continue to support these efforts. USAID is poised to support post-election reform efforts, assist the National Election Commission to apply lessons learned to further their capability, and professionalize political parties to further continue democratic development.

We will urge the newly elected Administration to consolidate democratic gains through effective and accountable governance, responsiveness to its citizens, and adherence to the rule of law. This includes developing and utilizing systems that reduce opportunities for corruption and waste of limited public resources. Our assistance will continue to promote good governance while strengthening critical public administration functions at national and local levels. These systems improve policy-making, budget and financial accounting, human resources management, and domestic revenue mobilization. We will continue to support land policy reforms and efforts to improve the quality of legal services available to the population, and we will build civil society and media oversight capacity, thereby reducing opportunities for renewed conflict or instability – key requirements for sustained peace and economic growth in Liberia.

Thank you Mr. Chairman, Ranking Member Bass, and members of the Subcommittee for the continued commitment you have shown to the Liberian people. I welcome any questions you might have.

———————

Mr. SMITH. Ms. Anderson, thank you very much for your testimony.

Just a few opening questions. One, you talked about the reports on the free election progress. Are those reports encouraging? Are they showing a willingness, for example, of the various candidates? I know State has met with the Liberian candidates to adhere to the rule of law. If they don't like the outcome, will they adhere to the outcome, providing it was free, fair, and transparent?

What have those reports suggested that we are on track for a good election or are there some warning signs?

Mr. YAMAMOTO. We have reporting coming in from Ambassador Christine Elder and her team, who have been in close contact with the National Electoral Commission and also with President Johnson Sirleaf, who has a big stake in ensuring the next elections are free, fair, and transparent and accountable to the people.

So far, everything looks on track. Obviously, from the Carter report, NDI report, and also our own reports there are challenges and problems ahead.

But overall, it looks to be on target. We have over 20,000, of course, poll workers are being trained through USAID and IFES and, of course, we are looking carefully at all of the over 5,360 polling areas to make sure that they are appropriate.

I think one of the big factors would be the rains—if it is raining, how people are going to get to the polling. That is going to be a challenge, given there are only 7 percent of paved roads in Liberia. But it is on target.

Mr. SMITH. Okay.

Let me ask you, with the U.N. Mission to Liberia, which we all know has played an integral part in disarming the more than 100,000 former combatants and has trained and professionalized Liberia's police force to ensure law and order and to advance women's participation in government and civil society, with UNMIL drawing down currently and on track to be entirely out next year, how prepared do you think the government will be. The bureaucracy and, of course, who heads the government will be extremely important to handle security on its own, especially since some of the candidates have poor records of human rights.

We don't know who's going to win. We don't take sides. But there is a concern—I have it at least and I am sure others do as well—about some people who have had very poor records of human rights who could be head of state.

Mr. YAMAMOTO. The program for UNMIL has been a success story and their extension past the election was really to ensure that there remains confidence in the process.

The issue is that it has been on target to remove—they have a token force now and I think they have done their mission and it is really up to the Liberian security forces.

In the last elections and currently, we assess that the defense force as well as the police still need training and guidance and mentoring. We will be on top of that with the 200 troops and over 600 police.

Our reports right now are that they are up to the target to meet the needs and, again, we will continue to be there. This remains a priority, even after UNMIL leaves.

Mr. SMITH. Let me just ask you briefly about the ability to register and vote. Are we convinced that the process is, again, transparent so that people who have signed up will find out when they show up at the polls there is their name, they can make their selection, and have confidence it will be counted correctly?

Ms. ANDERSON. I think we can be relatively optimistic now. We have been through the voter registration period with our support. I think we have seen fairly good turnout on the voter registration with an emphasis on hard to reach voters, first time voters, and also on women voters.

I can tell you that one of the kind of new technologies that we have supported is that Liberians can now use their cell phones, and many of them do have cell phones, and put in a message that includes their voter registration ID number and then get a message back that tells them where is the location for them to go and vote.

Mr. YAMAMOTO. And just to add to that, it is, again, the appeal process and we have been working very closely with President Johnson Sirleaf on the judicial process and due process, and if there are any problems from—expressed by the candidates on one of the candidates, then that will be addressed quickly and efficiently and effectively, we hope, and we will be there by the NEC and of also the judicial process.

Mr. SMITH. And last question before going to Ms. Bass. Ebola and the work that was done—just nothing but kudos for the great work that you did, the administration did, the military deployment, all of it was just textbook on how to try to mitigate a crisis from killing even more people.

We know Ebola is not gone. Are we convinced that we have early warning capabilities that, should it reemerge, that it could be quickly mitigated and hopefully eliminated?

Ms. ANDERSON. First of all, thank you for the generous support and guidance on the Ebola response. There hasn't been a new case in Liberia in 1½ years and we certainly recognize that countries with weak health systems and with low confidence in the public— in their public health systems that was where we had the big problems.

So this is no time for complacence. We have invested significant sources in the health systems and we are also building the citizens' confidence in their own services.

So I think there have been several recent outbreaks; Lassa fever and cholera where we were quite worried about spread and the Liberian public health system has been able to detect them through their surveillance system and successfully manage to control them.

So our efforts really are to help the public health system prevent, detect, and respond to disease and we will continue that.

Mr. YAMAMOTO. Mr. Chairman, I can't overemphasize the great work that you have done and, of course, Congresswoman Bass, because you have really highlighted a lot of the issues and challenges and really brought forth the things that we really need to focus on and it has really brought the international community focused on this and also all our groups.

And more important is the emphasis that you have all placed on institution-building, democratic values and really through this, strong institutions, we can guarantee and support anything that happens—pandemics or famines or other issues. And so thank you very much for your great work.

Mr. SMITH. Again, thank you, Mr. Ambassador and Ms. Anderson, for the great work you guys did. It is all about teamwork and I think this is one of those times where everyone came together and united to ensure that innocent people had not succumbed to that horrible and dreaded disease.

Ms. Bass.

Ms. BASS. Thank you, Mr. Chair.

And, actually, since you were talking about infrastructure, one, it is very good to hear that there has not been any new cases of Ebola.

When I was in Liberia in August of last year, they were concerned about relapse or it being transmitted after, you know, the fact. And so hearing that there haven't been any new cases is really good.

Not quite on our topic, but since you were talking about infrastructure, I was just wondering what more you think needs to be done now post-Ebola in terms of the health infrastructure.

Mr. YAMAMOTO. I defer to my colleague just on the basic programs that we are going to do on health. But I think overall it is simple things. The power generation, the MCC, and the $257 million in electrification.

You know, when we were out there in Liberia when Charles Taylor was transitioning out, there was no electricity and we were just amazed and shocked that this could ever happen. And it has, and thanks to you, the MCC program, et cetera.

The other issue, too, part of the MCC has been roads, really to bring the rural and the urban together but more important is to get access to those in rural areas, to bring them back for rapid treatment, et cetera.

So those are things to bring the country together and I think those are the infrastructure. The others are economic development and raising capacity building, particularly in the health sector.

I turn to my colleague on the other issue.

Ms. ANDERSON. I agree that our emphasis has to be on building local capacity so that Liberians can define their own future and their own path forward.

There is a lot more work to be done, obviously, in infrastructure and in the capacity and training of the individuals in the public health system, at the same time working to mitigate corruption and waste in governance and also building the capacity of Liberian institutions to hold their government accountable to the people.

Ms. BASS. Thank you. Thank you very much.

So I wanted to ask you now about U.S. Government assistance to Liberia, in particular in the area of good governance and democratization, and you could address that both from the USAID perspective and others.

So wanting you to describe the continuity and change in U.S. policy toward Liberia between our two administrations and what is proposed in the budget around democracy and governance and where we are, and if that has impacted what we are doing in Liberia today.

And I believe, Mr. Ambassador, you were mentioning poll workers that have been supported by our funding but I did not quite hear what you said in terms of the number.

Mr. YAMAMOTO. Yes. So right now, over 20,000 poll workers are being trained. Obviously, one of the problems for the NEC is to get numbers and also the training.

But I defer to USAID since it is coming from USAID and IFES.

Ms. BASS. Okay.

Ms. ANDERSON. We have a longstanding partnership with Liberia, and Liberia will continue to be a relative priority for us.

Democracy rights and governance is an important element of our programming in Liberia and it has really been an area of emphasis, working on governance, public financial management, building the capacity of the judiciary, working especially on anti-corruption, supporting civil society and the media, and our aim really, as I said, is a government that is responsive and accountable to its citizens and we will continue this into the next administration in Liberia.

Ms. BASS. So what concern that some of us have begun to have on the Hill is, one, there are the proposed cuts and, obviously, that is still working its way through the process, but whether or not in USAID you will be allowed to spend money that has already been allocated as opposed to slowing that process down because we have heard that in terms of the expenditures that are not being really implemented is one question. And I have a follow-up question to that.

Ms. ANDERSON. Yes. I think we are still continuing to be responsible for delivering development results with the funding that has already been appropriated and, as we go forward, if the levels are reduced we will just have to make sure that we are increasingly using our money more efficiently and more effectively.

Ms. BASS. And so you got what I was saying? I mean——

Ms. ANDERSON. Yes, I did.

Ms. BASS. Not the future. Money that is already there——

Ms. ANDERSON. Yes.

Ms. BASS [continuing]. And are you free to spend it? I don't know if you are involved at all with the famine effort. But we allocated close to $1 billion and we are hearing that that is being slow walked.

It is an emergency, and so is it getting out of the door or is it being held back and will it be carried over into the next fiscal year? I am saying that in reference to famine but we have heard that about the democracy funding as well.

Mr. YAMAMOTO. Can I have 1 more minute, Congresswoman?

So we have dedicated about $2 billion since 2003 and if you look at the last 10 years it is about $1.5 billion. But overall, the aid assistance, even toward the end of the last administration, was going down.

So the question comes in is, is for us we are looking at dwindling resources across the board but Liberia, for us, remains a priority country.

We still have, as you know, three bilateral commissions and, of course, Liberia becomes a fourth and that is critical and that is because of the work President Johnson Sirleaf has done and then all the good results she has gone through and we want continue that. So long as we are here, we are going to continue to commit to that. I mean, just looking to—at our own assistance as far as as-sistance to the military training, to other areas, yes, it is probably going to take some cuts. But the issue is that the commitment is still there and it continues into the next physical year.

I can't say what the amounts are going to be exactly. We will have to come back to you once those numbers are defined, but to assure you that for us, as long as we are here, that is a priority country.

Ms. BASS. Okay. So I hear you say that the commitment is there and commitment without resources is a little shallow.

But I also hear you saying that you are able to expend the money that is being allocated. Is the famine money spent?

Ms. ANDERSON. Yeah. I will——

Ms. BASS. I am sorry?

Ms. ANDERSON [continuing]. Be happy to get back to you on that.

Ms. BASS. Would you? I would appreciate that. I would appreciate that.

And so then my final question is what are we prepared to do after the election? I mean, as I mentioned, I was in Kenya and thought everything went well. Kind of went awry after the fact.

But it is one thing to get through the election. Then what are we prepared to do after the election?

Mr. YAMAMOTO. So the election is an event and from there comes really the hard work to ensure that the democratic procedures and processes that President Johnson Sirleaf has really put in efforts to during her two terms that they will continue—that we won't see a backtrack.

Then the other issue too is that we need to continue to strength-en the NEC, the legal process and procedures, because that is going to be very important to how we do the structures afterwards. And, again, we will be visiting Liberia constantly. Our Ambas-sadors will be committed. We are going to look at what we have to do—what areas do we need to emphasize and stress.

We are going to be continuing on MCC, Power Africa, and also the girls' education and women's entrepreneur, which is their two most important and, really, changing of society as a societal pro-gram.

And then we are going to look much more closely too at economic development to see how we can address the needs of the 50 percent youth and high unemployment rates in Liberia.

Mr. DONOVAN [presiding]. Thank you, Ms. Bass. Thank you, Mr. Ambassador. Thank you, Ms. Anderson.

Mr. Ambassador, State Department has met with the can-didates—the Liberian candidates that are running for election.

How confident are you that this relationship between our two countries will continue in the next government, particularly when you look at some of the human rights concerns that many Libe-rians have about some of the candidates?

Mr. YAMAMOTO. Like I said, in two ways. First are that the re-sults of those elections are by the people of Liberia themselves and

I don't think that the people of Liberia are ever going to go back to a
regression of what it was prior to President Johnson Sirleaf.
And the commitments and the developments that have been
made—I think the people are committed to those trend lines.

The second area, too, is that you have a large Liberian diaspora
in the United States. I think they are very vocal. They will keep
us on our toes if we are not focused on those issues, and my message to the—not only the diaspora—but the people of Liberia is
that we are still committed to ensuring that the results after the
elections will be as strong and as robust and continue because this
remains a priority country.

Mr. DONOVAN. Thank you.

Jewel Taylor, who is the former wife of Charles Taylor, current
senator and the Vice Presidential candidate, was reportedly in the
United States this year advocating for the release of her husband,
her ex—former husband from prison. Can you tell us what efforts
are being made about Charles Taylor's imprisonment and her efforts to have him released?

Mr. YAMAMOTO. You mean Charles Taylor, the——

Mr. DONOVAN. Yes.

Mr. YAMAMOTO. Okay. He is in jail for the long term. We have
not made any efforts to seek any change or adjustment to the due
process and what was adjudicated by the court systems.

Mr. DONOVAN. Okay. Had his wife met with folks from the State,
do you know, at all?

Mr. YAMAMOTO. We don't normally comment on——

Mr. DONOVAN. Okay.

Mr. YAMAMOTO [continuing]. People, but let me just say yes, we
did—we did meet with Jewel Howard Taylor and those conversa-
tions, I think, are between us.

Mr. DONOVAN. We totally understand, Mr. Ambassador. Thank
you.

Mr. YAMAMOTO. But, believe me, messages were passed.

Mr. DONOVAN. Great. Thank you.

Ms. Anderson, USAID is working with the international organizations such as the U.N. and other partners to ensure that the
election process in Liberia next month is smooth, credible, and
peaceful.

What more should the United States be doing, leveraging partnerships that we have with others to help ensure a successful outcome of the election?

Ms. ANDERSON. I think that coordination right now is very important and we are putting a big effort on coordinating our efforts
with others—other stakeholders in the process including other development partners, donors.

We—up until now, we are cautiously optimistic. We are reading
the reports that are coming in. I agree with Ambassador Yamamoto
that we are concerned about the logistics and the relatively weak
capacity of the Elections Commission.

It is still a work in progress, especially in light of the infrastructure and the rainy season. So one of the things that we have been
working on with the commission is communications because we
have seen in other elections sometimes that is where things break
down.

If there is a problem, if there is a delay, people start to get nervous and if the commission is not talking about what's happening, even if it is a mistake or a problem, that communication is very important.

So we have been working with them on that. At this point, I think maybe the only other thing I would mention would be there is a limited police presence outside of the capital, Monrovia, and we are keeping an eye on that.

The Liberian Government was asking for additional funding to be able to deploy the police that they have been training so that they can actually go out to the polling station locations. The Japanese Government recently put in a $1.1 million contribution to that.

Mr. DONOVAN. Thank you.

My last question is, I know USAID is managing two different programs on elections in Liberia, extending to next year. But at some point, those programs are going to end.

What is our confidence level that once those two programs' lifetime has expired the skills of the Liberian election officials to carry on all the work that you have done for all this length of time?

Ms. ANDERSON. I think you will hear more about that in the next panel with probably more detail than I can give. But our emphasis has been on building local capacity because it is the Liberians' responsibility to run their elections, to monitor them, and to participate in those elections.

So our emphasis has been on training and also anticipating problems to help the commission deal with issues before they escalate into big crises.

We will have to see what the future brings in terms of future elections.

Mr. DONOVAN. I thank you both, Mr. Ambassador and Ms. Anderson. I thank you for your testimony, your insight, and for your forthcoming answers to our questions.

This panel is now adjourned. We will give a 1-minute break to allow the next panel to come up. Thank you very much to both of you.

Ms. ANDERSON. Thank you.

Mr. DONOVAN. I would like to take a moment now to thank Chairman Smith and Ranking Member Bass for holding this hearing.

I would like to also welcome and thank all of our witnesses for being here today. I would especially like to welcome my constituent and good friend, Dr. Aurelia Curtis, along with her husband, Al, and her family.

Thank you for making this trip all the way down. Now you know what I go through every week.

I've known Dr. Curtis since my days of serving as chief of staff to then Staten Island Borough president, Guy Molinari, where she was then the principal of Curtis High School. That is how good we are in New York—we name our high schools after our principals. I asked Dr. Curtis to be a witness here today because of her unique perspective as someone who has been an integral part of the Liberian community in the United States.

For those of you who may not know it, Staten Island is home to the largest concentration of Liberians outside of Western Africa.

One of the many things that I have learned from Dr. Curtis and our local Liberian community is their dedication to highlighting the importance of freedom, liberty, and democracy, because they have seen first-hand the turbulence and chaos that arises when these principles are not upheld.

In recent years, Liberia has made strides in advancing its democratic and development efforts while we must recognize the challenges that we face ahead.

In less than a month, Liberia will hold elections that will test the nation's democratic strength and stability. This is an opportunity for the country to make history by allowing the Liberian people to experience their first post-war democratic transfer of power.

Looking to the future, it is this subcommittee's intention to ensure that Liberia is able to further build a strong, peaceful, and democratic nation.

We are fortunate to have a panel of experts including Dr. Curtis that will examine some of the issues I touched on as well as other important topics.

I look forward to hearing their insights as well as having thoughtful discussions to help put into place policies that will ensure Liberia's future as a stable democracy and strengthen the United States-Liberian relationships.

I now yield to the ranking member, Ms. Karen Bass.

Ms. BASS. Mr. Chair, I will defer my comments until the panel has spoken.

Mr. DONOVAN. Wonderful.

I would like to introduce our panel. David Peterson is senior director of the National Endowment for Democracy. Since 1988, he has been responsible for NED's program to identify and assist African NGOs.

He was formally executive director of Project South Africa of the A. Philip Randolph Education Fund and a freelance journalist in Africa and Turkey.

He has visited more than 40 African countries and is an expert in sub-Saharan Africa.

Dr. Aurelia Curtis is the founder of the Weeks Educational and Social Advocacy Project, Incorporated. It is based in Staten Island, New York, and Liberia.

As a key conduit between Liberia and the Liberian diaspora community in the United States, this agency's mission is to increase access to better education opportunities, expand social development, and improve health care for the community.

Dr. Curtis, as I said, was also the principal of Curtis High School in Staten Island, which has the largest concentration of Liberians outside of Western Africa.

Rushdi Nackerdien is the International Foundation Electoral Systems regional director for Africa. A founding member of what was the Electoral Leadership Institute, he was focused on electoral reform, capacity development, strategic planning, project and program evaluation, and expert advice in elections and development of e-learning materials with a special focus on Africa.

Additionally, he has guided the African Union in revising their election observation approach and has worked in numerous African countries such as Senegal, Ghana, and the Democratic Republic of Congo.

Dr. Chris Fomunyoh is the current senior associate and regional director of the Central and West Africa at the National Democratic Institute.

He has organized and advised international election observation missions and designed and supervised country-specific democratic support programs with civic organizations, political parties, and legislative bodies throughout Central and West Africa.

He recently designed and helped launch the African Statesman Initiative, a program aimed at facilitating political transitions in Africa by encouraging former democratic heads of state.

He is also an adjunct faculty—he is also an adjunct faculty member at the African Center for Strategic Studies and a former adjunct professor of African politics and government at Georgetown University.

On behalf of this subcommittee, I welcome you all. And at this point I recognize Mr. Peterson for his opening statement.

STATEMENT OF MR. DAVE PETERSON, SENIOR DIRECTOR, AFRICA PROGRAMS?, NATIONAL ENDOWMENT FOR DEMOCRACY

Mr. PETERSON. Thank you, Chairman Donovan and Ranking Member Bass. It is really a pleasure and an honor to be able to testify this afternoon.

Liberia has come a long way in the 30 years since the National Endowment for Democracy began working there in the waning years of the Samuel Doe regime, through the civil war, the interim government, the rule of Charles Taylor, and now two terms of Ellen Johnson Sirleaf, and the Ebola crisis.

Liberia's October 10 election should be competitive, peaceful, and democratic. But Liberia's democracy should not be taken for granted.

Having observed both the 1997 elections that brought Taylor to power as well as the 2005 elections that ushered in Ellen Johnson Sirleaf, I can testify to the determination Liberians have demonstrated for democracy at the ballot box.

According to Afrobarometer, 83 percent of Liberians support democratic elections. That is a very high level internationally.

The reports from our Liberian partners in the field describe lively candidate debates, successful voter registration efforts, massive civic education campaigns. They are mobilizing youth, women, traditional leaders, security forces, among others, to inform them about the process and the candidates and to participate responsibly.

They are using social media, phone banks, community town halls, radio, and even old-fashioned town criers to spread the word. They are monitoring the process, providing criticism and recommendations, and some are working directly to support the electoral commission.

According to one of our partners, campaigning has been peaceful and mature, even in the most troubled areas. As I say, candidates and their campaign managers have been keen on the issues and things they can do to improve livelihoods and environments of their people as opposed to indulging in ethnic politics.

Though we all know that democracy is more than elections and the challenges of governance in the interim can be daunting, predicting the future is dangerous, especially when it comes to the volatile politics of West Africa.

But Liberia could prove to be a reliable democratic partner of the United States. Its democratic institutions and popular commitment to democracy could grow stronger and its governance could improve.

How can this happen? Liberia is not the only country in West Africa holding democratic elections. Ghana's elections last year were a model of efficiency and transparency as well as being peaceful and democratic.

Gambia's elections last year were also competitive and produced a surprising transition. In the last few years, Senegal, Benin, Cote d'Ivoire, Burkina Faso, Mali, and, of course, Nigeria have held elections of varying quality but all essentially free and democratic.

Sierra Leone and Guinea will hold elections next year, which are also anticipated to be democratic. Thus, in this regional context, Liberia is fortunate to be surrounded by democratic-minded neighbors who are more likely to support Liberia's democratic trajectory than to divert it.

The kinds of cross-border attacks that used to occur back and forth between Guinea, Sierra Leone, and Cote d'Ivoire have ended. The steady withdrawal of U.N. and ECOWAS troops is not a sign of fatigue or diminished support but of confidence—that Liberia's own security institutions are strong enough to maintain order and protect the country.

All of these governments are friendly to the United States and as their democratic systems consolidate and mature, the entire West Africa region should come to be regarded as an important economic and political partner of the United States.

Liberia is special, as Congressman Smith has already noted. Although its population is only about 4.3 million, it is the only country in Africa that claims a special kinship to the United States—America's stepchild, as some Liberians put it.

Its history is closely intertwined with ours from the founding of the American Colonization Society in 1822, independence in 1847, the long dominance of the America Liberian elite, its service as an American base in World War II and the Cold War, to place names such as Monrovia, the Liberian flag, the uniquely American-accented Liberian English.

Liberians' political upheavals have brought waves of Liberian immigrants, as you've already noted, to the United States and, obviously, you are very familiar with their energetic lobbying for the issues that they are concerned about.

Most Liberians have long aspired for their nation to have a special relationship with the United States. Liberia's economic resources and commercial potential are also not to be dismissed, including rubber and palm oil, iron, tourism, and shipping.

I have run out of time. Whoever is elected President of Liberia will be keenly aware of these relationships and will likely want to strengthen them and take advantage of them. But the United States also stands to benefit from a strong, prosperous, and democratic Liberia.

In contrast to its destabilizing role in the region just 20 years ago, Liberia is now serving as a model for democratic transition, female leadership, and national reconciliation. In the struggle against extremists and criminal networks in West Africa, Liberia could prove particularly helpful.

Liberia's democratic institutions are in place and functioning but they need shoring up. The legislature, for example, is improving its performance, according to one of our partners that has been monitoring it for many years.

But it has not always shown the independence and integrity that Liberians expect. Only one-third of Liberian voters believe that members of their House of Representatives reflect their views, according to the Afrobarometer, and one of the popular issues in the campaign has been to cut legislators' rather generous salaries and benefits.

The legislative budget is almost equivalent to that of the entire education system in the country. Likewise, Liberia's judiciary remains weak.

The Supreme Court's recent rulings of the eligibility of certain candidates has stirred controversy and questions about its independence.

Having seen the critical role that the court played in the Kenyan elections, Liberians are skeptical that their own court would be able to show the same integrity.

Liberia's local justice structure suffers from a shortage of magistrates and lack of resources, police and prisons. Some Liberians have criticized the special court that tried Charles Taylor because their own justice system has received so little support.

I will leave the discussion about the Electoral Commission to my colleagues. I think they are better placed to comment on that. But it is an important institution.

I should just say that Liberia's press remains independent and lively despite resource problems. The anti-defamation cases have tapered off and a new freedom of information act has also been an important advance.

Civil society is very vibrant and often critical. It played a leading role in fighting Ebola and will continue to act as a watchdog as well as a partner with government when possible.

The labor movement and the business sector have been gaining strength and have been partners with our own Solidarity Center and Center for International Private Enterprise. These nongovernmental institutions are fundamental for the success of Liberian democracy.

Corruption, obviously, remains the weak point in Liberia's democracy, as for many African democracies. Nepotism, ethnic favoritism, shady contracts, vote buying, land deals, other forms of both grand and petty corruption can only undermine popular support for democracy and must be opposed.

Although the candidates in the election have expressed their readiness to fight corruption as has President Johnson Sirleaf herself, Liberians have seen very little progress.

Liberia must overcome many other challenges to consolidate its nascent democracy. The struggling economy, massive unemployment, dependence on the informal sector, ethnic conflict, religious conflict, land conflict, women's rights, environmental destruction—it is quite an agenda.

But I remain optimistic that with political will, popular commitment, and some modest assistance from international partners, Liberia can consolidate its democracy and steadily improve its governance.

Thank you. I look forward to your questions.

[The prepared statement of Mr. Peterson follows:]

**Testimony of Dave Peterson - National Endowment for Democracy
Hearing on the Future of Democracy and Governance in Liberia
House Foreign Affairs Committee, Subcommittee on Africa, Global Health,
Global Human Rights, and International Organizations
September 13, 2017**

Liberia has come a long way in the 30 years since the National Endowment for Democracy began working there in the waning years of the Samuel Doe regime, through the civil war, the interim government, the rule of Charles Taylor, and now the two terms of Ellen Johnson-Sirleaf and the Ebola crisis. Liberia's October 10 elections should be competitive, peaceful, and democratic. But Liberia's democracy should not be taken for granted.

Having observed both the 1997 elections that brought Taylor to power, as well as the 2005 elections that ushered in Ellen Johnson-Sirleaf, I can testify to the determination Liberians have demonstrated for democracy at the ballot box. According to the Afrobarometer, 83 percent of Liberians support democratic elections. The reports from our Liberian partners in the field describe lively candidate debates, successful voter registration efforts, and massive civic education campaigns. They are mobilizing women, youth, traditional leaders, and the security forces, among others, to inform them about the process and the candidates, and to participate responsibly. They are using social media, phone banks, community town halls, radio, and even old-fashioned town criers, to spread the word. They are monitoring the process, providing criticism and recommendations, and some are working directly to support the electoral commission. According to one NED partner, campaigning has been "peaceful" and "mature," even in the most troubled areas: "Candidates and their campaign managers have been keen on the issues and things they can do to improve the livelihoods and environments of their people as opposed to indulging into ethnic politics."

We all know that democracy is more than elections, however, and the challenges of governance in the interim can be daunting. Predicting the future is dangerous, especially when it comes to the volatile politics of West Africa; but Liberia could prove a reliable democratic partner of the United States, its democratic institutions and popular commitment to democracy could grow stronger, and its governance could improve.

How can this happen?

Liberia is not the only country in West Africa holding democratic elections. Ghana's elections last year were a model of efficiency and transparency, as well as being peaceful and democratic. The Gambia's elections last year were also competitive , and produced a surprising transition. In the last few years, Senegal, Benin, Cote d'Ivoire, Burkina Faso, Mali, and of course, Nigeria, have held elections of varying quality, but all essentially free and democratic. Sierra Leone and Guinea will hold elections next year, which are also anticipated to be democratic. Thus, in this regional context, Liberia is fortunate to be surrounded by democratic-minded neighbors who are more likely to support Liberia's democratic trajectory than to subvert it. The kinds of cross-border attacks that used to occur back and forth between Guinea, Sierra Leone, and Cote d'Ivoire have ended. The steady withdrawal of UN and ECOWAS troops is not a sign of fatigue or diminished support, but of confidence that Liberia's own security institutions are strong enough to maintain order and protect the country. All of these governments are friendly to the United States, and as their democratic systems consolidate and mature, the West Africa region should come to be regarded as an important economic and political partner of the US.

But Liberia is special. Although its population is only 4.3 million, it is the only country in Africa that claims a special kinship with the United States -- "America's Stepchild," as some Liberians put it. Its history is closely intertwined with ours, from the founding of the Liberian Colonial Society in 1846, the dominance of the Americo-Liberian elite, its service as an American base during World War II and the Cold War, to place-names such as Monrovia, the Liberian flag, and the uniquely American-accented Liberian English. Liberia's political upheavals have brought waves of Liberian immigrants to the US, and I know many Members of Congress are very familiar with the energetic lobbying of Liberian-Americans in your districts. Most Liberians have long aspired for their nation to have a special relationship with the United States, however wary they may be of the potential dangers. Liberia's economic resources and commercial potential are also not to be dismissed, including rubber and palm oil, iron, tourism and shipping. Whoever is elected president of Liberia will be keenly aware of these relationships, and will likely want to strengthen them and take advantage of them. But the United States also stands to benefit from a strong, prosperous, and democratic Liberia. In contrast to its destabilizing role in the region just 20 years ago, Liberia is now serving as a model for democratic transition, female leadership, and national reconciliation. In the struggle against extremist and criminal networks in the West Africa region, Liberia could prove particularly helpful.

Liberia's democratic institutions are in place and functioning, but they need shoring up. The legislature, for example, is improving its performance, according to one of NED's partners that has been monitoring the institution for many years, but it has not always showed the independence and integrity that Liberians would like. Only one-third of Liberian voters believe that members of the House of Representatives reflect their views, according to Afrobarometer, and one of the popular issues in the campaign has been the call to cut legislators' and government officials' salaries and benefits, which are indeed relatively high. The legislature's budget is almost equal to that of the entire education system.

Likewise, the judiciary remains weak. The Supreme Court's recent rulings on the eligibility of certain candidates has stirred controversy and questions about its independence. Having seen the critical role the Court played in the recent Kenyan elections, Liberians are skeptical that their court would be able to show the same integrity. Liberia's local justice structures are quite weak, suffering a shortage of magistrates and a lack of resources for police and prisons. Some Liberians have criticized the millions of dollars spent on the Special Court that tried Charles Taylor, when relatively little went to improve the justice system in local communities.

In a survey a couple years ago, Afrobarometer reported that only a third of Liberians trusted the National Elections Commission, but more recent reports from some of our partners suggest this has changed and that the NEC has been meeting its deadlines and is gaining the confidence of voters. I will leave my colleague from IFES to confirm this. But the bottom line is that Liberians are committed to democracy and the electoral process.

Liberia's press remains independent and lively, despite resource problems. Anti-defamation cases have tapered off, and a Freedom of Information Act was passed a few years ago, but the press will need to remain vigilant. Civil society is also vibrant and often critical. It played a leading role in fighting the Ebola epidemic; and will continue to act both as a watchdog, as well as a partner with government where possible. Both the labor movement and the business sector have been gaining strength in recent years, and both have benefited from partnerships with NED's core grantees, the Solidarity Center and the Center for International Private Enterprise. These non-governmental institutions are important foundations for Liberian democracy, and provide some hope that it is sustainable.

Corruption remains the weak point in Liberia's democracy, as is the case for many African democracies. Although the scale of corruption may be nowhere near that of Nigeria, the impact is just as destructive for Liberia. Nepotism, ethnic favoritism, shady contracts, vote-buying, land deals, and other forms of both grand and petty corruption can only undermine popular support for democracy. Although many of the candidates have expressed their readiness to fight corruption, as has President Johnson-Sirleaf, Liberians have seen little progress.

Liberia must overcome many other challenges to consolidate its nascent democracy. The struggling economy, massive unemployment and dependence on the informal sector, ethnic conflict, religious conflict, land conflict, women's rights, environmental destruction, and many other difficult problems will not be easily solved. Yet I remain optimistic that with political will, popular commitment, and some modest assistance from international partners, Liberia can consolidate its democracy and steadily improve its governance.

Mr. DONOVAN. Thank you, Mr. Peterson.

We are honored to be joined by Chairman Ed Royce, who is the chair of the Foreign Affairs Committee, which this subcommittee is part of.

The Chair now recognizes Dr. Curtis for her opening statement.

STATEMENT OF MS. AURELIA CURTIS, FOUNDER AND EXECUTIVE DIRECTOR, WEEKS EDUCATIONAL AND SOCIAL ADVOCACY PROJECT

Ms. CURTIS. Presiding chair, my Congressman Donovan, Ranking Member Bass, and members of the subcommittee, I thank you for the opportunity to provide testimony today about the role of the diaspora and Liberia's ongoing struggle for democracy.

The military coup in 1980, followed by the horrific civil war in 1989, which lasted almost 15 years, claimed hundreds of thousands of lives and significantly destroyed much of the infrastructure of Liberia.

A notable consequence of the war with the mass exodus of Liberians seeking refuge wherever doors were open, the United States of America opened its doors and the borough of Staten Island in New York City became home to the largest concentration of Liberians outside of West Africa.

The Staten Island diaspora remains the center of culture and connections for Liberians across the United States. Optimistic that we will be an integral part of the rebuilding of Liberia, ensuring that it is indeed a land of liberty. The past 12 years of peaceful governance is a foundation that all Liberians must build upon.

My name is Dr. Aurelia NdeKontee Louise Weeks Curtis and I serve as the executive director of the Weeks Educational and Social Advocacy Project, WESAP. I thank you, Congressman Donovan, for the gracious introduction.

I have worked for many nonprofit causes, but WESAP, with offices in the United States and Liberia, now claims most of my time and attention. WESAP has connected amputee children in Liberia with resources in the U.S., offering them prosthetic limbs.

When the children return to Liberia, WESAP ensures that they're enrolled in school, providing all tuition, fees, books, and uniforms.

A local social worker is a liaison between WESAP students and families, supporting youth development and other family needs.

WESAP has launched a campaign to put water wells near schools in Liberia that have no fresh water supply and is in partnership with two U.S.-based nonprofits to establish an all-girl boarding school in Liberia.

With the support of the Staten Island community, we assist families, especially immigrants and refugees from population groups that are not commonly represented in our area.

We provide multiethnic and culturally sensitive services that address their needs with respect and dignity. Recently, WESAP advocated for and assisted a family to return the mortal remains of their daughter to the United States for burial.

Princess Yates, a U.S. citizen born to Liberian parents on Staten Island, went to Liberia on July 4th to celebrate her grandmother's 90th birthday.

She was involved in a tragic automobile accident. According to published reports, the local hospital refused to give her needed medical assistance because money was not readily available to pay for treatment.

Her mother cried. Princess sat in an abandoned wheelchair, begging for help, until she took her last breath.

This incident highlights the critical need for timely access to good health care, especially in a country like Liberia with a high level of poverty whose infrastructure was decimated by the civil war.

Following the forthcoming elections, all Liberians must play a role indispensable to ensuring geometric growth in access to health care and other urgent facets of sustainable development in Liberia. Dual citizenship—Liberians in the diaspora often wonder if they are in fact welcome to participate in the rebuilding of Liberia. Pri‐ mary about stems from the lack of clarity regarding dual citizenship.

The Supreme Court of Liberia recently heard a case brought by Alvin Jalloh, a United States citizen born in Liberia to Liberian parents, who fled Liberia as a direct result of the civil war.

He emigrated to the United States and subsequently acquired U.S. citizenship in accordance with the naturalization laws of this country.

Chapter 22 of the Alien National—Alien and Nationality Law of Liberia "prohibits Liberian citizens from taking other nationalities or engaging in certain acts in foreign countries," including armed forces enlistments and participation in elections.

Liberians in the diaspora are watching this case closely because the wrong decision will have dire implications for the talent pool that is ready to return and assist in nation building.

A decision in this case has not been rendered. But wait. The Supreme Court may have already ruled in this matter when it failed to prevent several candidates in the forthcoming elections from contesting when evidence was presented to prove that said candidates had naturalized citizenship in other countries.

I call on this committee to use its influence to assist the people that you represent, Liberians in the United States of America, to attain dual citizenship, an initial hurdle that can be an impediment to tapping into the valuable human resource pool that resides outside of Liberia, a country in great need.

Liberians in the diaspora stand willing and ready to assist. But many are not prepared to abandon the country that gave them refuge in their time of need nor should they be forced to make such a decision.

DACA and TPS—temporary protective status for Liberia, Guinea, and Sierra Leone was terminated effective May 21st, 2017. Deferred action for childhood arrivals, DACA is being dismantled by the current administration.

Many immigrants, Liberians included, are adversely affected by the decision to end legal status, especially children who have known no other home than the United States of America. You have heard the appeals and protests to reinstate TPS and DACA.

I add my voice to the chorus of immigrants, highlighting the plight of thousands of law-abiding Liberians who have contributed to the economy of this country and call the U.S.A. home.

Please find a path for legal residence that will keep families united and offer students the opportunity to continue their education in the schools in which they are currently enrolled.

A house with two rooms—the final report of the Truth and Reconciliation Commission, TRC, of Liberia Diaspora Project documents the experience of human rights abuses and violations of international humanitarian law that force Liberians to leave the country.

The Staten Island Liberian Community Association and Staten Island-based African Refuge supported the work of the advocates for human rights to document this dark time in Liberian history. Based on analyses of more than 1,600 statements, interviews, and witness testimonies, the TRC report tells the stories of trauma experienced by members of the diaspora during the flight through Liberia and across international borders and in resettlement in the United States and United Kingdom.

My father was among those who walked for days, sometimes sleeping under open skies, to escape warring factions. His home was taken over by rebels.

Even after he found his way out of Liberia and into the United States, he continued to suffer the recollection of atrocities. The awful ramifications of Alzheimer's disease did not curb his desire to return to his home that he was forced to leave by rebel combatants.

While many in the diaspora will attribute the beginning of Liberia's civil crises to the 1979 riots, I believe that there were many telling signs before April 1979.

Poverty, political dominance, corruption, tribalism, and low literacy were significant contributors. Those political landmines did not begin in 1979. The same themes were present in interviews, the witness testimonies from members of the diaspora.

The themes persist today and reared their ugly heads when I spoke informally to members of the community as I prepared for this testimony.

The civil war has left entrenched resentments and divisions along tribal and political lines—evidenced in the diaspora, ever present in current campaign rhetoric. There is no quick solution to problems resulting from more than 100 years of dysfunction in government and social practices.

The TRC report was a necessary start. Ignoring the TRC report adds fuel to the fire and buffers the rhetoric of many who believe there is no room at the table for them. So for many it is time to turn the table upside down.

We cannot and must not allow stagnation to steer us backwards. Liberians on Staten Island and across the diaspora recognize the need for reconciliation and healing the wounds of the Liberian nation.

When President Johnson Sirleaf inaugurated the TRC she said, "Our country cannot continue to evade justice and the protection of human rights throughout our land, especially the kind that restores our historical place among civilized nations. Our Government will ensure that those culpable of the commission of crimes against humanity will face up to the their crimes no matter when, where, or how."

The current government has not dealt decisively with the TRC report. So the next government elected in October or November 2017 must chart a transparent course of action.

The TRC report will not fade away into oblivion. No one disputes the findings, even though two commissioners did not sign the report because of undocumented dissenting views. The Liberian Government must determine if it will implement all or some of the recommendations.

A new commission must be inaugurated to provide a timetable for implementation. The new TRC must have the benefit of using the investigative body that prepared the report as a resource.

The mandate to develop a plausible plan for dealing with the recommendation made almost 8 years ago must be front and center in the first 100 days of the next government. Rethinking governance with hearts in mind, Liberians in the diaspora agree that rebuilding the physical and human capital must be top priorities for the next government.

The close links between infrastructure development, education, agriculture, and health care are indisputable. There is no substitute for establishing desired goals and planning for how one will achieve those goals.

Simplistic as it may sound, planning works. We call on the next government to share the 1-year, 3-year, 5-year, and 10-year plans for four key areas—infrastructure development, education, agriculture, and health care.

Integrated in the plan must be measures on accountability and quality control. If it is not working, the government must be prepared to revise the plan to ensure that the established goals are achieved.

The socioeconomic schisms in Liberia are more pronounced than they were 12 years ago. How do we know that? Follow the money. Money transfer companies are sending large sums of money from the diaspora to support families in Liberia. But transfers are also going in the other direction, from Liberia to banking institutions overseas.

Please explain to me how it is possible for anyone employed by the world's third poorest nation to legally amass enough wealth to build homes locally, buy homes overseas, and still have change to spare.

I call on this committee to ensure that pressure is brought to bear on the Government of Liberia to institute systems that prevent and prosecute corruption all levels.

In my other life, I would tell exam proctors your job is to prevent cheating, not to catch cheaters. Similarly so, the Government of Liberia must make it difficult for corruption to persist, and when corruption is uncovered, effective prosecution must send a strong message that a government for, of, and by the people will not stand by idly while the people are disenfranchised.

[The prepared statement of Ms. Curtis follows:]

Written Testimony of Dr. Aurelia L. Curtis
Founder and Executive Director
Weeks Educational and Social Advocacy Project, Inc. (WESAP)
Before the House Subcommittee for
Africa, Global Human Rights, Global Health & International Organizations

SUBJECT: The Future of Democracy and Governance in Liberia

Wednesday, September 13, 2017, 2:00 pm

Chairman Smith, Ranking Member Bass, Congressman Donovan and Members of the Subcommittee, I thank you for the opportunity to provide testimony today about the future of democracy and governance in Liberia. The military coup in 1980, followed by the horrific civil war in 1989 which lasted almost 15 years, claimed hundreds of thousands of lives and significantly destroyed much of the infrastructure of Liberia. A notable consequence of the war was the mass exodus of Liberians seeking refuge wherever doors were open. The United States of America opened its doors and the Borough of Staten Island in New York City became home to the largest concentration of Liberians outside of West Africa. The Staten Island Diaspora remains the center of culture and connections for Liberians across the United States, optimistic that we will be an integral part of the rebuilding of Liberia, ensuring that it is indeed a "Land of Liberty." The past 12 years of peaceful governance is a foundation that all Liberians must build upon.

My name is Dr. Aurelia TdeKontee Louise Curtis, and I serve as the Executive Director of the Weeks Educational and Social Advocacy Project, Inc. (WESAP), a nonprofit founded in 2010 with the mission of increasing access to better education opportunities, expanding youth development and improving healthcare in needy communities. I began my professional career in the New York City public schools in 1984 as a Teacher of Mathematics and Computer Science and retired in 2015 as Principal of Curtis High School on Staten Island. I was the first African-American to be named principal of a high school on Staten Island and the first female principal of Curtis High School in its more than one hundred year history. As principal of Curtis High School, I served a diverse immigrant community that included a large number of Liberian families in the Diaspora.

I have worked for many nonprofit causes, but WESAP, with offices in the United States and Liberia, now claims most of my time and attention. WESAP has connected amputee children in Liberia with resources in the US, offering them prosthetic limbs. When the children return to Liberia, WESAP ensures that they are enrolled in school, providing all tuition fees, books and uniforms. A local social worker is a liaison between WESAP, students and families, supporting youth development and other family needs. WESAP has launched a campaign to put water wells near schools in Liberia that have no freshwater supply and is in partnership with two US-based nonprofits to establish an all-girl boarding school in Liberia. With the support of the Staten Island community, we assist families, especially immigrants and refugees from population groups that are not commonly represented in our area. We provide multi-ethnic and culturally-sensitive services that address their needs with respect and dignity. Recently, WESAP advocated for and assisted a family to return the mortal remains of their daughter to the United States for burial. Princess Yates, a US citizen born to Liberian parents on Staten Island, went to Liberia on July 4th to celebrate her grandmother's 90th birthday. She was involved in a tragic automobile accident and, according to published reports, the local hospital REFUSED to give her needed medical assistance because money was not readily available to pay for treatment. Her mother cried, "Princess sat in an abandoned wheelchair begging for help until she took her last breath!" This incident highlights the critical need for timely access to good healthcare, especially in a country like Liberia with a high level of poverty, whose infrastructure was decimated by the civil war. Following the forthcoming elections, all Liberians must play a role indispensable to ensuring geometric growth in access to healthcare and other urgent facets of sustainable development in Liberia.

Dual Citizenship

Liberians in the Diaspora often wonder if they are in fact welcome to participate in the rebuilding of Liberia. Primary doubt stems from lack of clarity regarding dual citizenship. The Supreme Court of Liberia recently heard a case brought by Alvin Jalloh, a United States citizen born in Liberia to Liberian parents, who fled Liberia as a direct result of the civil war. He immigrated to the United States and subsequently acquired US citizenship in accordance with the naturalization laws of this country. When he applied for a Liberian passport, he was denied the travel document because he is an American citizen. Chapter 22 of the Alien and Nationality Law of Liberia "prohibits Liberian citizens from taking other nationalities or engaging in [certain acts] in foreign countries," including armed forces enlistment and participation in elections. Liberians in the Diaspora are watching this case closely because the wrong decision will have dire implications for the talent pool that is ready to return and assist in nation building. A decision in this case has not been rendered. But wait! The Supreme Court may have already ruled in this matter when it failed to prevent several candidates in the forthcoming elections from contesting when evidence was presented to prove that said candidates had naturalized citizenship in other countries. I call on this subcommittee to use its influence to assist the people that you represent, Liberians in the United States of America, to attain dual citizenship, an initial hurdle that can be an impediment to tapping into the valuable human resource pool that resides outside of Liberia, a country in great need. Liberians in the Diaspora stand willing and ready to assist, but many are not prepared to abandon the countries that gave them refuge in their time of need; nor should they be forced to make such decision.

DACA and TPS

Temporary Protected Status (TPS) for Liberia, Guinea and Sierra Leone was terminated effective May 21, 2017. Deferred Action for Childhood Arrivals (DACA) is being dismantled by the current administration. Many immigrants, Liberians included are adversely affected by the decision to end legal status, especially children who have known no other home than the United States of America. You have heard the appeals and protests to reinstate TPS and DACA. I add my voice to the chorus of immigrants, highlighting the plight of thousands of law-abiding Liberians who have contributed to the economy of this country and call the USA home. Please find a path to legal residence that will keep families united and offer students the opportunity to continue their education in the schools in which they are currently enrolled.

A House with Two Rooms

The final report of the Truth and Reconciliation Commission (TRC) of Liberia Diaspora Project documents the experience of human rights abuses and violations of international humanitarian law that forced Liberians to leave the country. The Staten Island Liberian Community Association (SILCA) and Staten Island based African Refuge supported the work of The Advocates for Human Rights to document this dark time in Liberian history.

Based on analyses of more than 1600 statements, interviews and witness testimonies, the TRC report tells the stories of trauma experienced by members of the Diaspora during their flight through Liberia and across international borders and in resettlement in the United States and United Kingdom. My father was among those who walked for days, sometimes sleeping under open skies to escape warring factions. His home was taken over by rebel forces. Even after he found his way out of Liberia and into the United States, he continued to suffer the recollection of atrocities. The awful ramifications of Alzheimer's disease did not curb his desire to return to his home that he was forced to leave by rebel combatants.

While many in the Diaspora will attribute the beginning of Liberia's civil crises to the 1979 rice riots, I believe that there were many telling signs before April 1979. Poverty, political dominance, corruption, tribalism and low literacy were significant contributors. Those political landmines did not begin in 1979. The same themes were present in interviews and witness testimonies from members of the Diaspora. The themes persist today and reared their ugly heads when I spoke informally to members of the community as I prepared for this testimony. The civil war has left entrenched resentments and divisions along tribal and political lines, evident in the Diaspora and ever-present in current campaign rhetoric.

There is no quick solution to problems resulting from more than one hundred years of dysfunction in government and social practices. The TRC report was a necessary start. Ignoring the TRC report adds fuel to the fire and buffers the rhetoric of many who believe there is no room at the table for them; so for many, it's time to turn the table upside-down! We cannot and must not allow stagnation to steer us backwards. Liberians on Staten Island and across the Diaspora recognize the need for reconciliation and healing the wounds of the Liberian nation.

When President Johnson-Sirleaf inaugurated the TRC she said, "Our country cannot continue to evade justice and the protection of human rights throughout our land, especially of the kind that restores our historical place among civilized nations. Our Government will ensure that those culpable of the commission of crimes against humanity will face up to their crimes no matter when, where, or how." The current government has not dealt decisively with the TRC Report; so, the next government elected in October or November 2017 must chart a transparent course of action. The TRC report will not fade away into oblivion. No one disputes the findings even though two commissioners did not sign the report because of undocumented dissenting views. The Liberian government must determine if it will implement all or some of the recommendations. A new commission must be inaugurated to provide a timetable for implementation. The new TRC must have the benefit of using the investigative body that prepared the report as a resource. The mandate to develop a plausible plan for dealing with the recommendations made almost eight years ago must be front and center in the first 100 days of the next government.

Rethinking Governance with Heart and Mind

Liberians in the Diaspora agree that rebuilding the physical and human capital must be top priorities for the next government. The close links between infrastructure development, education, agriculture and healthcare are indisputable. There is no substitute for establishing desired goals and planning for how one will achieve those goals. Simplistic as it may sound, planning works! We call on the next government to share the one-year, three year, five-year and ten-year plans for four key areas: infrastructure development, education, agriculture and healthcare. Integrated in the plans must be measures of accountability and quality control. If it is not working, the government must be prepared to revise the plan to ensure that the established goals are achieved.

The socio-economic schisms in Liberia are more pronounced today than they were 12 years ago. How do we know that? Follow the money. Money transfer companies are sending large sums of money from the Diaspora to support families in Liberia. But, transfers are also going in the other direction - from Liberia to banking institutions overseas. Please explain to me how it is possible for anyone employed by the world's third poorest nation to legally amass enough wealth to build homes locally, buy homes overseas and still have change to spare! I call on this committee to ensure that pressure is brought to bear on the Government of Liberia to institute systems that prevent and prosecute corruption at all levels. In my other life I would tell exam proctors, "Your job is to prevent cheating, not to catch cheaters!" Similarly so, the Government of Liberia must make it difficult for corruption to persist and when corruption is uncovered, effective prosecution must send the strong message that a government for, of and by the people will not stand by idly while the people are disenfranchised.

How do we reduce poverty when the disparity in salary compensation is so evident? Why are members of the Liberian legislature, in a poor country with limited budgetary resources, given such high monthly salaries and benefits, competitive with those of members of the U.S. Congress, when their constituents can barely afford daily sustenance? (Annual Salary of a Member of the House of Representatives in Liberia: $172,104 plus expenses; Annual Salary of a Member of the US Congress: $174,000 plus benefits) How will education and healthcare improve when these professionals are among the lowest paid in the country? (Average annual salary of a teacher: $3,840; average annual salary of a nurse: $4,200; Average annual salary of a medical doctor: $24,000) Why can a government-run medical facility refuse care to a patient because there are no funds for registration and there is no legal recourse? These are but a few of the questions that must tug at the heart of those called to lead Liberia.

Summary
The literal translation of my name, TdeKontee, in Bassa (my mother's Liberian language), is "everything has its time." When I was born, it was time for my parents to have their first girl and the promises to be fulfilled in her coming. TdeKontee! It is time for the crawling democracy in Liberia to dare to walk.

The consolidated final report of the Truth and Reconciliation Commission is dedicated to the "evergreen memory of all those who lost their lives during the Liberian conflict, the Children of Tomorrow and ALL who dare to HOPE for a better Liberia!" Liberians residing on the mother soil dare to hope for a better Liberia. Liberians in the Diaspora dare to hope for a better Liberia. Ladies and gentlemen of the subcommittee on Africa, Global Human Rights, Global Health & International Organizations, I believe that you dare to hope for a better Liberia. So, I call on you to act decisively to ensure that dual citizenship for Liberians in the Diaspora becomes a reality; chart a course to legal residence for law-abiding undocumented immigrants; demand with conviction that the four years of work of the TRC is not placed on the back burner and ignored, thus assuring that the collective expressions and recommendations contained in that document are translated into actionable steps in the next Liberian administration to continue the healing process; continue to assist Liberians to improve systems of governance and accountability for sustainable progress in infrastructure and economic development, agriculture, education and healthcare reform.

Chairman Smith, Ranking Member Bass, Congressman Donovan and Members of the Subcommittee, I thank you again for the opportunity to provide testimony today. I will be happy to answer your questions.

References

http://www.frontpageafricaonline.com/index.php/news/4160-supreme-court-of-liberia-hears-argument-on-dual-citizenship

http://www.theadvocatesforhumanrights.org/uploads/a_house_with_two_rooms.pdf

http://www.fahnbulleh.net/docs/trc_final_report.pdf

https://mfdp.gov.lr/index.php/the-budget#

http://allafrica.com/stories/201702200408.html

Mr. DONOVAN. Thank you, Dr. Curtis.

We are going to enter the rest of your testimony into the official record and take up some of those issues during the question and answer period.

Ms. CURTIS. I apologize if I——

Mr. DONOVAN. No, that is okay. You are very passionate about this. Thank you, Dr. Curtis.

We are going to take a pause for a moment. Chairman Royce has another hearing that he has to attend so the Chair recognizes Chairman Royce.

Chairman ROYCE. Well, thank you, Mr. Chairman, very much.

We have got a very long history of ties to Liberia, going back to July 26th of 1847. We know it is July 26th because that is Greg Simpkins's birthday here and he's the staff director and he and I have worked on Liberian issues since the '90s.

And so there have been some disappointments. We were trying to get information into Liberia so that in her first race, Ellen Johnson Sirleaf could compete with Charles Taylor in the election.

But he controlled all of the media and as a consequence, of course, he won. We were very disappointed, as you can imagine, afterwards to see what happened in Liberia with the mutilations and the murder rate and everything that transpired not only there but in neighboring Sierra Leone.

For a while, one of the young men who worked in my office was a survivor. He lost both of his parents. He was from Sierra Leone. But he lost both of his parents to an attack by the Revolutionary United Front, and that group, of course, had been supported again by Charles Taylor. So it was very bad time for West Africa.

When I chaired the Africa Subcommittee, we worked very diligently across party lines to send a clear unified message and that Charles Taylor needed to be brought to the bar of justice, and against the odds, he was.

We have a respite here and in the meantime, years later, we have seen some impressive growth in Liberia. I have been out to Liberia and seen a number of the steps that are being taken and I got to tell you, the U.S. has invested there to rebuild and support democratic institutions, and as a nation confronted with immense political and economic and, of course, security and development challenges, Liberia has persevered.

And I would just take for a moment the time to say that, in my view, President Ellen Johnson Sirleaf has been leading these efforts and I commend her strong leadership through two terms.

But she is stepping down from office, and I think this is admirable because she is setting an example for other African leaders now in terms of stepping down and giving an opportunity for the next person to run for President in an open election.

I think those elections provide an opportunity to consolidate these democratic gains. It is a peaceful transfer of power. If done successfully, Liberia will be a model to fledgling democracies across Africa.

And on that, I want to thank the members of this committee because I think the members here—your continued interest in this, your efforts to help this along—will have very, very consequential impacts.

I see Al White's in the audience. He is the former chief investigator of the Sierra Leone special court.

And again, for those of you who have kept this interest, you know, for a generation, it is important. A steady hand—a steady hand of assistance here is important.

The fact that the Liberian diaspora community—the American Liberian community—is so involved is a huge asset to the people of Liberia.

So as we look ahead to future engagement, we all recognize one thing and that is that deep reforms are needed to further address corruption.

In Liberia, just like the rest of the world, this is something that has to be confronted and a more conducive environment for trade and for business investment is really needed.

So we here in the United States have got to remain a willing partner to support this transition of power where the will of the people is respected and upheld and beyond so that our country, the ancestral home of many Americans, our country and Liberia, can together continue to push for this hopeful track.

We have a special responsibility here as Americans, and for the Liberian-American community here, thank you again for your engagement. Let us try to be clear-eyed. Let us make certain that there is accountability.

Let us make certain we are on the ground in order to check in terms of the elections. I am going to meet—I am meeting here momentarily with the head of IRI and DNI.

We have got to make sure, you know, that all these steps are taken and that we want to continue to help with reforms and we insist on the inclusion of the Liberian American community.

Thank you very much for the time here, Chairman.

Mr. DONOVAN. Thank you, Mr. Chairman.

We will resume with opening statements. The Chair now recognizes Mr. Nackerdien for his opening statement.

STATEMENT OF MR. RUSHDI NACKERDIEN, REGIONAL DIRECTOR FOR AFRICA, INTERNATIONAL FOUNDATION FOR ELECTORAL SYSTEMS

Mr. NACKERDIEN. Thank you, Mr. Chairman.

Mr. Chairman, Ranking Member Bass, and distinguished members of the subcommittee, on behalf of the International Foundation for Electoral Systems, I deeply appreciate this opportunity to discuss the evolution of Liberia's democracy.

With generous backing from USAID and international partners, IFES supports credible electoral processes globally.

In many parts of the world including Liberia, IFES works with its partners in the Consortium for Elections and Political Process. Strengthening the International Republican Institute and the National Democratic Institute.

Mr. Chairman, credible elections strengthen peace and democracy. This is no truer than in Liberia.

Twelve years ago with the 2005 elections, Liberia was emerging from a civil war, a war that left hundreds of thousands dead, disabled, or displaced, a war wracked with the use of child soldiers and an epidemic of violence against women.

The 2005 election shattered a double glass ceiling, leading to the first elected female head of state in Africa and the first black woman head of state, Her Excellency, Ellen Johnson Sirleaf.

On October 10th, 2017, Liberians will recommit to democracy, as Johnson Sirleaf is ineligible to run for a third term and should be congratulated for honouring her country's constitutional term limits.

This election will mark the first democratic transfer of political power in Liberian history.

IFES has implemented election programs in Liberia since 2004. Over time, our work has become more focused and nuanced.

In 2005, Liberia's National Election Commission, known as the NEC, relied heavily on the U.N. peacekeeping mission and IFES. In 2011, it began standing independently. In 2014, in the midst of the Ebola crisis, the NEC ably conducted special senatorial elections.

This is progress and it relied on IFES support in several key areas such as voter registration, results management, campaign finance, and electoral dispute resolution.

Mr. Chairman, our efforts are yielding results. A recent survey found that 91 percent of Liberians feel free to choose whom to vote for while 90 percent feel free to join any political organization.

The NEC increased its voters register from 2014 to 2017 by 15 percent to 2 million registered voters. With IFES support, the NEC registered 67 percent of young voters.

A 2017 USAID-funded study found that the majority of Liberians interviewed trust the NEC as an impartial and transparent body. In sum, without U.S. support, the commission would be weaker, less prepared for the elections, less voters would be registered, and less would know about the process, and the October elections in Liberia would be more expensive.

For instance, the Government of Liberia assessed the viability of biometric voter registration for the upcoming elections. IFES advised against its implementation prior to the coming elections, citing cost and logistical reasons.

The government agreed with our assessment and did not attempt a premature or rushed implementation of new untested technology. This is a clear example of how mutual trust both over time and adherence to local context leads to cost effective and practical decisions that can stave off electoral mishaps.

Despite this progress, the NEC faces several challenges. Liberia's road network, already unreliable, will lengthen the delivery and retrieval of electoral materials, especially during the height of rainy season.

The core of election officials still depend on continued international support for both planning and implementation. A run-off election is a highly likely scenario.

The NEC will have 2 weeks after the announcement of the first round results for administering a runoff. This will strain the systems. These challenges highlight the continued need for assistance, which brings me, Mr. Chairman, to my recommendations for the U.S. Congress.

Firstly, I thank the U.S. Congress for its robust bipartisan funding of democracy assistance and also its continued support.

Electoral assistance as evidenced in Liberia with Liberia's success should start early and continue through the post-election period to allow for flexible and responsive programming.

Multi-year multi-election programs are the most impactful. In Liberia, we recommend continued support to a possible constitutional referendum to the eventual introduction of biometric voter identification and registration and to the strengthening of judicial capacities.

Mr. Chairman, thank you again for this opportunity to testify. The October 2017 elections will be landmark achievement for Liberians and we congratulate them in advance.

I am happy to answer any questions you might have.

[The prepared statement of Mr. Nackerdien follows:]

The Future of Democracy and Governance in Liberia

Testimony of Rushdi Nackerdien
Regional Director Africa, International Foundation for Electoral Systems (IFES)

House Committee on Foreign Affairs
Subcommittee on Africa, Global Health, Global Human Rights,
and International Organizations

September 13, 2017

Testimony of Rushdi Nackerdien,
Regional Director, Africa, International Foundation for Electoral Systems

"The Future of Democracy and Governance in Liberia"

House Committee on Foreign Affairs
Subcommittee on Africa, Global Health, Global Human Rights, and International Organizations

September 13, 2017

Mr. Chairman, Ranking Member Bass, and distinguished members of the Subcommittee: on behalf of the International Foundation for Electoral Systems (IFES), I deeply appreciate this opportunity to discuss the evolution of Liberia's democracy, in the context of its electoral process.

Since 1987, IFES has worked in over 145 countries to support citizens' right to participate in free, fair, transparent and accountable elections. IFES provides technical assistance to strengthen local capacity and electoral inclusiveness in societies that aspire to realize their full democratic potential. Stable democracies make for better trading partners, provide new market opportunities, improve global health outcomes, and promote economic freedom and regional security.

In addition to our current work in Liberia, IFES has empowered individuals and those institutions that make democracy work at every phase of the electoral cycle in Africa in countries such as Burkina Faso, Burundi, the Central African Republic, Côte d'Ivoire, Guinea, Kenya, Liberia, Mali, Nigeria, Sierra Leone, Uganda, Zimbabwe and others.

With support from the United States Agency for International Development (USAID) and numerous international partners – including the United Kingdom's Department for International Development, Global Affairs Canada, the United Nations Development Programme (UNDP), and the European Union (EU) – IFES has supported credible, free, and fair electoral processes in roughly half the countries across the sub-region. In many parts of the world, including Liberia, IFES also works with its Consortium for Elections and Political Process Strengthening (CEPPS) partners – the International Republican Institute and the National Democratic Institute   under USAID's Global Elections and Political Transitions mechanism on comprehensive democracy, human rights, and governance programming. IFES programs deliver expert technical assistance to help all electoral stakeholders participate in, plan for and administer inclusive political processes across the electoral cycle, from legal framework reforms, to voter registration, to civic education, the elections themselves, and results management beyond elections.

IFES' Sub-Saharan African programs utilize generous donor support to strengthen both sides of the democracy scale: 1) Supply – in the form of credible political processes, administered by professional and independent institutions; and 2) Demand – in the form of an activated citizenry with protected rights and full access to the systems that impact their lives. IFES positions itself at the center of this equation, partnering with all electoral stakeholders to strengthen participation, transparency, responsiveness, and ultimately democratic performance. As a rule, the dynamism of all societies produces social and political changes that often outpace the ability of governments to respond in a timely and comprehensive manner. This is perhaps truer in Sub-Saharan Africa than anywhere else in the world.

Electoral Assistance: A Long-term Development Commitment

Figure 1: The Electoral Cycle

No team makes it to a championship without hard work in the pre- and regular seasons, as well as some intense post-season analysis and rebuilding. Similarly, although Election Day may be the "Super Bowl" of the electoral cycle (see Figure 1), it is simply one event in a long process.

To this end, effective electoral assistance demands investment several years in advance of an election date and in the period between elections. At the heart of a strong electoral cycle is the professionalism of the electoral management body (EMB) and an empowered civil society.

Consistent, long-term support throughout the electoral cycle also enhances stability during uncertain democracy building processes. Shorter term or immediate assistance does not allow for capacity building, the introduction of technology (or the training and public education necessitated by it), or strategic planning.

The Liberian Electoral Context

Non-indigenous Americo-Liberians dominated Liberian politics between independence in 1847 and 1980; in fact, the country's first 10 presidents were born in the United States. In 1980, a military coup led by Samuel Doe ousted President William Tolbert and effectively ended the First Republic. However, the Doe administration's perceived favoritism for the Krahn ethnic group gradually generated widespread tensions across Liberia, particularly after he was formally elected president in 1985. In 1989, a militia led by Charles Taylor invaded Liberia from Côte d'Ivoire, sparking a conflict that would grow to span two largescale, devastating civil wars involving a variety of factions until the Economic Community of West African States brokered a ceasefire in 2003.

Following the 2003 Comprehensive Peace Agreement (CPA) and the cessation of conflict, Liberia held landmark elections in 2005 that saw the election of Her Excellency Ellen Johnson-Sirleaf. The elections broke a long-standing double glass-ceiling, resulting in the first elected female head of state in Africa and the first black woman head of state. These breakthrough elections were made possible through large-scale support of the international community, particularly through international peacekeeping forces led by the United Nations Mission in Liberia (UNMIL),[1] as well as with support and technical expertise provided by IFES with generous funding from USAID.

The United States-Liberia relationship runs deep – Liberia supported the United States during World War II, and served as a bulwark for American interests during the Cold War. In modern times, the U.S.-Liberian

---

[1] United Nations Security Council Resolution 1509 (2003), September 19, 2003. See https://www.un.org/en/ga/search/view_doc.asp?symbol=S/RES/1509(2003)&referer=https://www.un.org/en/pea cekeeping/missions/unmil/resolutions.shtml&Lang=E

relationship has evolved into one of critical strategic importance. For example, our countries successfully partnered to contain Ebola and prevent it from reaching our shores in a significant way, and Liberia is a key trading partner of the United States – Liberia's U.S.-owned-and-operated shipping and corporate registry is the world's second-largest.[2]

Mr. Chairman, Liberia is on the verge of consolidating hard-fought democratic gains. However, from the perspective of a democracy with free and fair elections, Liberia has only recently emerged from a long history of single-party rule. There is much work to be done.

Governance and Election Management Architecture

Liberia's government is comprised of executive, legislative, and judicial branches. The bicameral legislative branch consists of a Senate and a House of Representatives. There are 30 senators and 73 members of the House of Representatives, with two senators and a minimum of two representatives from each of Liberia's 15 counties. At present, senators serve a nine-year term and representatives serve a six-year term. President Johnson-Sirleaf is presently serving her second (six-year) term in office and is ineligible to seek re-election in October 2017. The highest judicial body in Liberia is the Supreme Court, and includes five justices nominated by the president. The Senate must confirm each justice's life-long tenure.

Liberia's National Elections Commission (NEC) represents an autonomous public commission responsible for conducting elections for all elective public offices and administering and enforcing all elections laws. Established under Article 89 of Liberia's 1986 constitution, the NEC has undergone a number of changes over the years, transforming from the Elections Commission (ECOM) in 1986 to the reconstituted NEC in the 2003 CPA, which ended 14 years of conflict in Liberia. The NEC has been responsible for major general elections in 2005 and 2011, the 2011 constitutional referendum, and the 2014 special senatorial elections – which it administered during the Ebola crisis. At present, seven administrators manage the NEC, including a chair, co-chair and five commissioners. With the Senate's advice and consent, the president appoints each to a seven-year term.

Although the NEC officially administered the 2005 and 2011 general elections, the international community provided extensive financial, technical and logistical support. For example, for the 2005 election, UNMIL brought an electoral division into Liberia with a budget of approximately $19 million. These funds were raised and made available through a collaborative arrangement between the NEC, the UN, IFES, the European Community and the UNDP, to cover NEC operations and the elections.[3]

---

[2] "U.S. Relations with Liberia," U.S. Department of State Fact Sheet. August 29, 2017. See https://www.state.gov/r/pa/ei/bgn/6618.htm

[3] UNDP (2010). *The Longer Term Impact of UNDP Electoral Assistance: Lesson Learned.* Available at: http://toolkit-elections.unteamworks.org/?q=webfm_send/541

Subsequent to the 2005 elections, UNMIL withdrew its electoral capacity to the NEC and formally handed over its electoral portfolio to the UNDP.[4] The UNDP then assumed responsibility for the 2011 election.[5]

Several electoral assessment missions in Liberia in 2009 culminated in the 2010-2012 "Liberian Electoral Cycle Project," through which the UNDP provided technical assistance to the NEC with a basket fund budget of over $27 million used to update Liberia's voters' roll, undertake voter registration, empower government institutions and civil society organizations, train women aspirants in political participation, fund civic education, hold a national referendum on matters relating to elections, and procure, distribute and retrieve electoral materials for the October 2011 elections and November second-round run-off.[6] Major funders included the EU and the governments of Denmark, Germany, Japan, Spain and Sweden.

However, an audit of UNMIL electoral assistance activities in Liberia between 2009 and 2011 deemed that the mission only partially fulfilled its mandate.[7] Specifically, the audit found that although UNMIL assisted Liberia in its preparation for the presidential and legislative elections, it did not establish its electoral assistance capacity in a timely manner, and its electoral assistance strategy and plan of action was not in place until April 2011.

U.S. Government Support to Liberian Elections

The U.S. Government has consistently supported Liberia since its post-conflict transition. Following the signing of Liberia's 2003 CPA, IFES conducted a field assessment of the NEC; these results formed the basis of a five-year program in Liberia, which began in November 2004. Through the follow-on program from 2009-2014, IFES developed sound working relationships with local election officials and civil society organizations that increased local ownership and cultivated domestic confidence in the NEC's capacity, transparency and impartiality. IFES implemented this follow-on program, "Building Sustainable Elections Management in Liberia," with $18.8 million in USAID funding. The program provided technical and material assistance to develop the NEC's capacity in several key election management areas including voter registration, civic and voter education, public outreach, legal reform and public information. IFES also played a major role in conducting civic and voter education for voter registration, the 2011 national referendum and the general and run-off elections. The program also produced three voter education films that were shown throughout the country in "mobile-cinemas," reaching hundreds of thousands of voters with consistent and useful information.

---

[4] Overall results relating to UNMIL's effective implementation of its electoral assistance mandate were partially satisfactory (October 21. 2011). Available at:
https://usun.state.gov/sites/default/files/organization_pdf/186051.pdf
[5] UNDP (2010). *The Longer Term Impact of UNDP Electoral Assistance: Lesson Learned*. Available at: http://toolkit-elections.unteamworks.org/?q=webfm_send/541
[6] UNDP. *UNDP Liberia Annual Report 2011*. Available at:
http://www.undp.org/content/dam/liberia/docs/docs/UNDP%20in%20Liberia%20Annual_Report_2011.pdf
[7] *Overall results relating to UNMIL's effective implementation of its electoral assistance mandate were partially satisfactory* (October 21, 2011). Available at:
https://usun.state.gov/sites/default/files/organization_pdf/186051.pdf

With almost $12 million in USAID funding through the CEPPS mechanism, IFES started its current "Liberia Elections and Political Transition" program in January 2015, with the goal of developing a cadre of election officials capable of managing the full electoral cycle by 2019. To achieve this, IFES is providing strategic learning opportunities, such as Building Resources in Democracy, Governance and Elections (BRIDGE)[8] workshops, campaign finance regulations and monitoring training, as well as tailored trainings in electoral dispute resolution procedures and regulations for magistrates. Additionally, IFES has conducted and utilized an evaluation of the NEC – along with the NEC's current strategic plan (mid-term evaluation and revision supported by IFES) – to elaborate specific program activities that have been and continue to be jointly identified and prioritized to maximize institutional strengthening. Among the initiatives conducted to date are focused learning opportunities for NEC staff and magistrates, such as technical assessment and improvement of information and communication technology management capacities, technical support on electoral legal framework management, the development of a persons with disabilities inclusion policy, graphic design assistance and training for voter registration and elections activities and materials (including ballot papers), long-term mass communications outreach support, and the development of social media outreach tools, including two nationally-broadcast radio programs and revised website design.

IFES has also provided more than $1.5 million in commodity support directly and indirectly to the NEC, including the printing of civic and voter education materials, hardware and software for the Data Center, increased electoral awareness through national and interactive radio broadcasting, diesel generators and internet connectivity for each of the 19 magisterial offices, and a hybrid battery bank that provides uninterrupted power to the Data Center. Without this support, the total number of registered voters would be lower, the public's level of electoral awareness would not be as acute, and the NEC would not be as prepared as it is today to administer the October 2017 elections.

The Impact of Electoral Support

IFES, alongside UNMIL, UNDP and other international partners, has continued its support to Liberian electoral processes up to the present, assisting the NEC in creating its own track record of credible elections in 2011 and 2014. IFES' technical and material support to Liberia's electoral processes has been critical to the country's democratic evolution, and gives insight into the challenges and opportunities ahead. A recent Afrobarometer report[9] found that 91 percent of Liberians feel free to choose who to vote for, while 90 percent feel free to join any political organization they wish. Furthermore, Liberians have seen an increase in their levels of trust in the NEC. Freedom House rates Liberia as "Partially Free," with a score of 62 out of 100.[10]

A 2017 study conducted with USAID funding indicated that, the majority of Liberians interviewed, trust the NEC as an impartial and transparent body, which supports the 14.7 percent increase in voter

---

[8] BRIDGE is an internationally-recognized training curriculum co-founded by IFES, the UNDP, the Australian Electoral Commission and International IDEA; for more information please see http://www.bridgeproject.org/en/

[9] Afrobarometer Dispatch 121, October 2016; see http://afrobarometer.org/publications/liberia-round-6-summary-results-2015

[10] https://freedomhouse.org/report/freedom-world/2017/liberia

registration since 2014. Of the 2.18 million registered voters, 67 percent are between the ages of 18-37, indicating that the NEC's civic and voter education strategy, which was revised with IFES' support, has been effective in engaging Liberia's largest demographic sector. IFES' technical support to the NEC has had other tangible results, as revealed in a 2015 survey funded by USAID,[11] which found that 82 percent of those surveyed correctly identified their polling place as their registration center, that nearly 75 percent recalled seeing or hearing NEC messages urging them to register or explain how to register to vote, and over 75 percent evaluated the NEC's performance as "good" with regard to educating citizens how to register to vote. More recently, IFES' input to a white paper requested by the Government of Liberia regarding biometric voter registration influenced the determination that, while plausible, it was neither a feasible, nor practical endeavor prior to the October 2017 elections, due to cost and logistical considerations.

With the upcoming October, 2017 general elections, Liberia has the opportunity to consolidate its democratic gains. As incumbent President Johnson-Sirleaf is ineligible to run for a third term, this election will mark the first democratic transfer of political power in Liberian history. While there were a variety of transitional transfers of power between the CPA in 2003 and the inauguration of President Johnson-Sirleaf, they took place in an immediate post-conflict setting with a large peacekeeping presence, and the leaders were not democratically elected but served transitional roles. The upcoming elections will be administered without the widespread peacekeeping forces of UNMIL, as the electoral security responsibilities nationwide has been handed over to the Liberia National Police.

Upcoming Electoral Challenges
On Election Day – October 10, 2017 – Liberians will recommit to democracy. Having learned from the technical expertise provided by organizations such as IFES, the NEC has a far greater institutional capacity to conduct nationwide elections than in either 2005 or 2011. Among the improvements include a demonstrable commitment to public engagement and communications, a more robust approach to results tabulation and management, greater appreciation and awareness of gender inclusion and ensuring equal access for persons with disabilities, and stronger in-house training capacities. However, despite this organizational progress, the NEC will face several challenges in the conduct of the October 2017 general elections.

Only 54 percent of Liberians viewed the 2011 national elections as completely free and or with minor problems, yet 78 percent of Liberians felt the 2014 special senatorial elections, conducted on the heels of the Ebola virus crisis, were completely free and fair or with minor problems.[12] Logistical challenges remain great, particularly in the absence of UNMIL peacekeeping forces that played a large role in transportation of electoral materials throughout the country in previous elections. The condition of Liberia's road network, while improving, remains fragmented and unreliable outside of a few major inter-city networks. Exacerbating this challenge is the fact that the elections will take place during the height of the country's rainy season, further deteriorating road conditions and lengthening transportation and travel timelines.

---

[11] See http://pdf.usaid.gov/pdf_docs/PA00KJW1.pdf
[12] *Ibid.*

The NEC has thus far met its planned electoral deadlines, and has set a strong foundation for the potential conduct of credible elections. However, with 5,390 polling stations spread throughout rural areas of the country's 19 electoral districts, logistical and transportation challenges remain an obstacle to be overcome. The NEC has planned for these challenges, and procured all-terrain vehicles and trucks, and has the option to hire private helicopters should that become necessary in the absence of sufficient UNMIL support.

An additional question is whether voter turnout will be adequate for elections inclusive of a large portion of Liberian citizens. Based on voter turnout from past presidential and general elections in 2005 and 2011, a turnout (in round one) of up to 80 percent is anticipated (compared to a turnout of about 60 percent for the United States' 2016 elections[13]). However, if there is torrential rain in many areas of the country on Election Day, it will have a direct impact on the willingness and ability of Liberians to reach their polling stations (sometimes up to 10 kilometers away, through difficult terrain).

Should it be necessary, the NEC is required to administer a second round (run-off) two weeks following the announcement of round one's final results. Both the 2005 and 2011 elections featured a second-round election for the presidency, and in both cases turnout was markedly lower. In 2005, second-round voter turnout dropped to 62 percent from 76 percent in the first round. In 2011, the second-round voter turnout was only 39 percent, down from 72 percent in the first round. With IFES' support, the NEC has developed contingency plans for a 2017 run-off. A run-off is a distinct possibility, given the high number of presidential candidates.

These challenges also highlight the need for the assistance of IFES and international partners. IFES has been instrumental in building the capacity of the NEC's Civic and Voter Education Section, providing training and technical advice about how to reach rural voters with effective messaging, as well as messaging specifically targeted at reaching women and persons with disabilities. Nearly 75 percent of the country's voting population resides outside of Monrovia, and many primarily communicate in a language other than English, so special emphasis must be placed on conveying messages in the appropriate language or dialect. Through IFES programming, supported by USAID, public service announcements related to elections are broadcast nationally in five major languages. As such, IFES continues to supplement civic awareness outreach throughout rural areas through funding local civil society organizations in coordination with regional NEC offices.

Competent election personnel are a critical element of any successful election. In addition to building the capacity of NEC staff in Monrovia, IFES has conducted training programs for election magistrates and assistant magistrates throughout the country to ensure that regional support complements competent national leadership. In addition, IFES has supported the NEC's training of temporary staff; in 2017, the NEC will hire and train some 27,000 temporary poll workers. Despite international support, and the NEC's

---

[13] "2016 November General Election Turnout Rates," United States Elections Project. See
http://www.electproject.org/2016g

experience conducting elections in 2005, 2011 and 2014, literacy and educational challenges that require additional attention persist. Even though the NEC is a permanent body, efforts to build a cadre of core technical and administrative staff capable of administering all phases of the electoral cycle independent of significant international assistance require continued support.

Conclusion

Liberia will continue to consolidate its gains as a democratic state and society through the upcoming election and political transition. The gradual strengthening of Liberia's electoral processes will generate second-order effects vital to the country's on-going recovery from two civil wars, the last of which ended less than 15 years ago.

Strong democracies are less prone to internal or external events capable of destabilizing or otherwise disrupting progress in areas such as economic growth, and service delivery of public healthcare and education. Liberia's ability to conduct senatorial elections in the wake of the 2014 Ebola crisis is an indication not only of the NEC's improved performance capacity, but also of its resolve to uphold its constitutional mandate. The October 2017 general and presidential elections will be a landmark achievement for Liberia, as they will not only confirm the country's determination for a peaceful and democratic political transition, but they will further instill public trust in those institutions responsible for upholding inclusive, democratic systems. Aside from solidifying peace, and the benefits of a democratically elected government and the implications for freedom for the citizenry, foreign investment would likely increase, improving the economy, and providing greater resources for the improvement of living conditions, health systems, and educational resources.

The United States has played a critical role in Liberia's post-conflict recovery through a myriad of direct and indirect inputs in diverse areas such as agriculture, education, healthcare, and vocational training, to name a few. The success of these vital socio-economic recovery and development platforms ultimately depends on the strength of Liberia's public institutions, which are themselves a function of participatory governance. Without a strong and confident elections management mechanism, no country can aspire to greater prosperity. Elections are not just episodic events; they are the temporary culmination of years of planning and preparation during the electoral cycle. Prematurely withdrawing or even curtailing election management support for Liberia would stifle its trajectory at a critical period in its growth since October 10, 2005. As with efforts to address corruption, improve government accountability, and strengthen the social contract through the provision of greater services, developing capable election management systems requires a long-term vision.

Although the new government will bring new approaches to Liberia's existing problems, it will also encounter new challenges. The United Nations' commendable tenure in Liberia is gradually coming to an end, as exemplified by the phase out of peacekeeping operations and diminishing financial support for elections. Continued U.S. Government support of good governance initiatives will therefore soon be even more critical to Liberia's continued emergence from the post-conflict era.

IFES is proud of its accomplishments since 2005, but there remain some areas of electoral management where continued and targeted support is necessary, including the possibility of conducting a constitutional referendum, the desired introduction of biometric voter identification and registration, and strengthened magisterial capacities.

Mr. Chairman, thank you for the opportunity to present IFES' views about the future of democracy in Liberia, a progression in which we are proud to have played a role through building the capacity of Liberia's National Elections Commission.

INTERNATIONAL FOUNDATION FOR ELECTORAL SYSTEMS
IFES
30 Years
Global Expertise. Local Solutions.
Sustainable Democracy.

Mr. DONOVAN. Thank you very much.

The Chair now recognizes Dr. Fomunyoh.

STATEMENT OF CHRISTOPHER FOMUNYOH, PH.D., SENIOR AS-SOCIATE AND REGIONAL DIRECTOR FOR CENTRAL AND WEST AFRICA, NATIONAL DEMOCRATIC INSTITUTE

Mr. FOMUNYOH. Mr. Chairman, Ranking Member Bass, distinguished members of the subcommittee, on behalf of the National Democratic Institute, NDI, I appreciate the opportunity to discuss prospects for advancing democracy and good governance in Liberia following next month's elections.

I focus on the elections because how they are conducted will have significant impact on the legitimacy of the ensuing government and legislature and the performance of governance institutions.

On October 10th, Liberians will go to the polls to elect a President, Vice President, and 73 Members of the House of Representatives.

There are 20 Presidential and Vice Presidential tickets and approximately 1,000 candidates for seats in the House of Representatives.

Since 2003, NDI has, with funding from the U.S. Agency for International Development and the Swedish Government, worked to strengthen the development of democratic institutions and practices in Liberia.

To support Liberian efforts to conduct credible polls in 2017, NDI deployed two pre-election assessment missions to Monrovia in February and September, currently has long-term observers and analysts in country, and will deploy an international election observation mission for the October polls.

The institute is also providing technical assistance to a coalition of civil society organizations, the elections coordinating committee. They have plans to deploy thousands of citizen observers to monitor the polls across all 15 counties of the country.

Furthermore, NDI is training party poll watchers from all political parties on how to enhance transparency by monitoring all aspects of voting on behalf of their candidates and collecting evidence from polling stations to use in the electoral disputes resolution process should the outcome of the polls be contested.

Liberia has enjoyed a continuous period of 14 years of peace since the end of armed conflict in 2003 and citizens aspire to building a resilient democracy that delivers for its people.

The upcoming elections will mark an historic milestone for the country as they present an opportunity for the first peaceful transfer of power from one elected President to another since 1944.

According to recent focus groups undertaken by NDI, Liberians are enthusiastic about the elections and have faith in their ability to determine the outcome.

They home that candidates and political parties present policy proposals during the ongoing campaign so citizens can make informed choices.

The recent focus group research also underscored the fact that Liberians embrace democracy not only as a means to end conflict but also as the governance model that fosters accountability so governing institutions can deliver on citizens' expectations.

Should the elected leaders be unable to satisfy these expectations, citizens may lose faith in democracy and further disengage from the political process, hence reinforcing apathy and stalling the country's democratic progress.

With the election campaign underway, Liberians repeatedly stated to NDI observers that they, and I quote, "do not want their communities to revert to the armed conflicts of decades past."

The future of democracy in Liberia will hinge in the short term on the perceived success of failure of the October polls and in the long term on the ability of future leaders to consolidate the games that have been made in the last decade in improving governance and meeting citizens' demands.

If voters have confidence that the electoral process is fair and credible and that their collective will is reflected in the outcome, that will go a long way in laying the foundation for greater stability, peace, and sustainable development.

In my full written statement, I discuss in more detail the electoral process and future prospects in the post-election period with regards to specific entities and issues, notably, the executive and legislative branches of government, security sector performance, civil society, decentralization, and the rule of law.

I would like to submit that full statement as well as the September 9th statement issued by NDI's pre-election assistant mission for the record.

I thank you for your time and look forward to your questions.

[The prepared statement of Mr. Fomunyoh follows:]

Statement by Christopher Fomunyoh, Ph.D.
Senior Associate and Regional Director for Central and West Africa
National Democratic Institute

Before the U.S. House of Representatives Committee on Foreign Affairs
Subcommittee on Africa, Global Health, Global Human Rights,
and International Organizations

The Future of Democracy and Governance in Liberia

September 13, 2017

Mr. Chairman, ranking member Bass, and distinguished members of the Subcommittee, on behalf of the National Democratic Institute (NDI), I appreciate the opportunity to discuss prospects for advancing democracy and good governance in Liberia following next month's elections. I focus on the elections because how they are conducted will have significant impact on the legitimacy of the ensuing government and legislature, and the performance of governance institutions.

On October 10, Liberians will go to the polls to elect a president, vice president, and 73 members of the House of Representatives. There are 20 presidential/vice presidential tickets and approximately 1,000 candidates for seats in the House of Representatives.

Since 2003, the National Democratic Institute (NDI) has, with funding from the U.S. Agency for International Development and the Swedish International Development Cooperation Agency, worked to strengthen the development of democratic institutions and practices in Liberia. To support Liberian efforts to conduct credible polls in 2017, NDI deployed two pre-election assessment missions to Monrovia in February and September, currently has long term observers and analysts in-country, and will deploy an international election observation mission for the October polls. The Institute is also providing technical assistance to a coalition of civil society organizations -- the Elections Coordinating Committee -- that plans to deploy thousands of citizen observers to monitor the polls across all 15 counties of the country. Furthermore, NDI is training party poll watchers from all political parties on how to enhance transparency by monitoring all aspects of voting on behalf of their candidates and collecting evidence from polling stations to use in the electoral dispute resolution process, should the outcome of the polls be contested.

Introduction
The upcoming elections will mark an historic milestone for the country, as they present an opportunity for the first peaceful transfer of power from one elected president to another since 1944. According to recent focus group studies undertaken by NDI, Liberians are enthusiastic about the elections and have faith in their ability to determine the outcome. They hope that candidates and political parties present policy proposals during the ongoing campaign so citizens can make informed choices. The country has enjoyed a continuous period of 14 years of peace since the end of armed conflict in 2003, and citizens aspire to build a resilient democracy that delivers for its people.

Recent focus group research also underscored the fact that Liberians embrace democracy not only as a means to end conflict, but also as a governance model that fosters accountability so governing institutions can deliver on citizen expectations. Should elected leaders be unable to satisfy these expectations, citizens may lose faith in democracy and further disengage from the political process, hence reinforcing apathy and stalling the country's democratic progress. With the election campaign underway, Liberians repeatedly state to NDI observers that they "do not want their communities to revert to the armed conflicts of decades past."

If properly organized, the upcoming elections would lend legitimacy to the government that emerges, empower legislators to more forcefully exercise proper oversight and better represent constituents, and create new opportunities for citizens to contribute to the consolidation of peace and stability.

The future of democracy in Liberia will hinge, in the short-term, on the perceived success or failure of the October polls and in the long-term, on the ability of future leaders to consolidate the gains that have been made in the last decade in improving governance and meeting citizen demands. If voters have confidence that the electoral process is fair and credible and that their collective will is reflected in the outcome, that would go a long way in laying the foundation for greater stability, peace, and sustainable development.

Electoral Process
NDI just conducted a pre-election assessment mission to Liberia from September 3-9, following an earlier mission conducted in February. Overall, the findings of the just completed mission give room for guarded optimism in Liberia's ability to conduct meaningful polls. Liberians are enthusiastic about the elections and, so far, have faith that their votes will determine the outcome. Prospects for credible polls are bolstered by several factors: incumbent President Ellen Johnson Sirleaf is stepping down at the end of her term as stipulated by the constitution (as opposed to some African leaders that have amended constitutions to remain in power); the presidential race is open and competitive, with 20 registered candidates; the campaign has thus far been peaceful, with parties and candidates pledging to avoid actions that could undermine peaceful and inclusive polls; and the National Elections Commission (NEC) is viewed favorably by most stakeholders.

Nonetheless, some challenges remain, including: concerns over whether the voter register will contain the names of all Liberians that registered to vote; the timeliness of electoral preparations, notably the delivery and deployment of voting materials; and divergent interpretations of recent NEC and Supreme Court decisions. The statement by NDI's assessment mission explores these issues in more detail and offers recommendations that, if implemented, would enhance confidence in the electoral process. *I would like to submit the mission's full statement for the record.*

Liberians interviewed by NDI focus groups are hopeful about the future, if the elections are conducted well. These prospective voters view the polls as a catalyst for the improvement of their well-being that could further nourish the country's rebirth or renewal. They are fearful of renewed conflict, economic decline, and physical insecurity, should the elections fail.

Post-Election Transition and Future Prospects
While most Liberians seemed to understand that the current administration had been saddled with the burdens of national reconciliation and reconstruction after a devastating civil war, they are likely to place higher expectations on the next administration for more efficient service delivery and further strengthening of governance institutions.

In 2015, Afrobarometer surveys showed that more than 50 percent of Liberians are not satisfied with the state of democracy in their country, with 77 percent of those interviewed feeling that the members of the House of Representatives never or only sometimes listen to what citizens say. The report also found that most Liberians do not feel that elected officials work for them or represent their interests. This finding explains the large turnover in the House following the 2011 and 2014 legislative polls. In July 2016, a focus group report by NDI showed similar dissatisfaction, particularly among women and youth, many of whom felt excluded from the governance process.

On governance indicators such as perceptions of corruption, nepotism, and government ineffectiveness, the 2015 Afrobarometer survey found that 65 percent of Liberians believed that most or all government officials and legislators are corrupt. Moreover, in 2016, a Global Witness report linked some officials and legislators to a bribery scandal in the mining sector.

Executive Branch
While the current administration engaged early on in a constitutional reform process, the constitutionally mandated time for such reform falls outside of the October 10 timeframe. Hopefully, the next administration will embrace the reforms identified so far, and lead the constitutional reform process to its conclusion.

The country faces challenges with poor infrastructure (particularly in rural areas), slow macroeconomic trends, low literacy rates, and difficult living conditions for many of its citizens. Liberians hope for progress on these priority issues. To govern effectively, the new government will have to rigorously pursue innovative policies in these areas.

The absence of infrastructure not only impacts negatively on living conditions for citizens; it also impedes their ability to engage in democratic processes, such as interacting with elected representatives and national institutions based in the capital city and participating in activities such as voter registration and voting. Some communities in rural areas do not have easy access to information, and hence may register lower participation rates in the elections.

Decentralization
While a national consensus seems to have developed in the last decade on the need to devolve power and public resources to counties and districts, early efforts at decentralization have not been completed. The next government will have to accelerate governance reforms that would provide citizens at the local level opportunities to make decisions that impact their daily lives. Decentralization often serves as an incubator for better service delivery. It can also spur infrastructural development which, in the specific case of Liberia, is lacking or rudimentary outside of the capital city of Monrovia.

Security Sector Performance
As a post-conflict country, since 2003 Liberia received significant financial, logistical, and security support from the international community to run its elections. The October 2017 polls will be the first national elections to be run almost exclusively by Liberians with minimal technical assistance from the international community. Notably, this would be the first time since 2003 that Liberian security services will provide election security independent of the United Nations peacekeeping operation (UNMIL). Although some Liberians with whom our delegation met expressed skepticism about the ability of the Liberian National Police (LNP) to provide the necessary security for the elections, others are confident of the LNP's capacity to perform its mission. So far, the LNP is viewed positively by political parties and other stakeholders for its proactive communication, trust-building approach, and emphasis on community policing. Citizen observer groups also view the LNP positively, and praise the professionalism of its members during the first month of campaigning. An Electoral Security Task Force has been set up, as well as a coordination mechanism that allows the UN Police to provide guidance and technical advice to the LNP, if needed.

Under its 2017 Election Security Plan, the LNP will work closely with other Liberian uniformed services, such as the Bureau of Immigration and Naturalization, the Drug Enforcement Agency, and the Liberia National Fire Service, to deploy more than 7,300 officers countrywide to guarantee security during the polls. A Police Special Unit and an Election Response Unit will be deployed in the eight counties identified by the LNP as "hot spots." Special escort guards have also been trained by the LNP to secure all election materials, and security details have been assigned to each presidential candidate.

Liberia's Legislature
Although the Liberian legislature has made efforts to increase its effectiveness during the past decade, more would have to be done by the new legislature to overcome lingering negative perceptions of that institution by citizens. In particular, the next legislature will have to embrace the constitutional reform agenda. It will also need to enhance its inclusiveness by creating leadership opportunities for women members.

After record high participation as voters and candidates during the 2005 elections that culminated in the election of a woman head of state -- the first female African president -- the percentage of Liberian women on voter rolls has dropped in subsequent years. Low literacy rates and cultural and financial barriers inhibit the ability of Liberian women to participate in elections as voters, candidates, and poll workers. Currently, only 10 percent of Liberia's elected representatives are women. The election law was amended in 2014 to include a stipulation that political parties "should endeavor" to reach at least 30 percent women on their candidate lists. However, female candidates represent less than 16 percent of the total number of registered candidates for the upcoming elections. Only one out of 26 political parties -- the Liberia Restoration Party (LRP) -- reached the 30 percent benchmark. The LRP is also the only party to nominate a female presidential candidate. Three political parties -- Alternative National Congress (ANC), All Liberia Party (ALP), and Unity Party (UP) -- have between 14 and 20 percent representation of women candidates.

Rule of Law
In recent months, the NEC and the Supreme Court issued rulings that were criticized by segments of the Liberian population. While some analysts argue for a liberal interpretation of the law and various guidelines in order to foster inclusiveness in a post-conflict setting, the NEC and the Supreme Court would have to ensure that election-related disputes are resolved expeditiously, and in a manner that engenders public confidence in the judicial process. Over the longer-term, the Liberian government will have to undertake reform to harmonize the legal framework of elections in the country in order to further strengthen the rule of law.

Civil Society
Liberian civil society and independent media are quite vibrant during this electoral period. Two major civil society coalitions -- the Elections Coordinating Committee (ECC) and Liberia Election Observers Network (LEON) -- will deploy thousands of citizen observers across the country to monitor the polls. Other organizations have engaged in intensive civic and voter education and get-out-the-vote initiatives for women and other marginalized groups. These organizations will gain new skills in advocacy and civic organizing and mobilization that could be transformed into continued advocacy on governance, transparency, and accountability in the post-election period.

Conclusion
While the country has made great strides since the end of civil war in 2003, Liberians recognize that peace is fragile. Therefore, the stakes are high for the upcoming elections. The new government and legislature will have to respond to citizens' expectations, encourage citizen engagement and inclusive political participation, fight corruption, and continue and deepen the reform process to focus on public policy issues about which citizens care the most.

Mr. DONOVAN. I thank you very much, all of you, for your opening statements. I will take a few moments to ask some questions and then Ranking Member Bass will ask her questions.

Mr. Peterson, there is an international polling organization—it may have been Afrobarometer—that reported that Liberians have more faith in the National Election Commission and the selection than they have in the past.

Is there anything to attribute that confidence in? Has anything changed that confidence in our own election process?

Mr. PETERSON. Well, I think the commission has had some time to improve its operations. IFES, of course, has been working very closely with them for some years now.

The Afrobarometer poll, as you note, a couple years ago was finding that only about a third of Liberians had, you know, significant trust in the electoral commission.

But from what our partners are telling us now, you know, people are pretty confident that the commission can do its job. But I think there has been a lot that has been invested in the commission. It has got, you know, decent independent leadership and that makes a big difference.

Mr. DONOVAN. Thank you.

Dr. Curtis, that beautiful young lady from Staten Island who went back home—back to Liberia, suffered from that great loss, the accident in which she was denied medical care, is that the norm really?

Is that—is that what happens to people in Liberia who can't pay for medical care and is there anything that our country is doing about that?

Ms. CURTIS. I think there is a lot that United States of America is doing about it. Knights of America has been a good friend to Liberia.

The development of Liberia over the last 12 years would not have been possible without the friendship and the support of the Knights of America, the government, the institutions here, the USAID.

But we have a broken system. We have a broken health care system that requires quite a bit. We have a broken education system, and the—as I said in my statement, while the last 12 years of governance have been a great foundation that we can build on, there is still much to be done.

Infrastructure development, education, health care reform, and paying attention to agriculture, which is what most Liberians know how to do, are going to be key challenges for the next government.

There is so much at stake in this next election, and as a Liberian in diaspora I am grateful that Liberia has the United States as a partner in this and as a guide to help with establishing accountability and—for in areas that we are not historically good at.

Mr. DONOVAN. Your advocacy for dual citizenship—do the Liberians back in Liberia, would they welcome American Liberians going there and participating in the election process or would they feel that there is an interference from outside sources if we—if more and more people were involved with dual citizenship?

Ms. CURTIS. I have heard arguments on both sides. But I tell you, Congressman, that in this election there is evidence that there are at least two candidates that have said they have citizenship in other countries.

So will Liberians welcome them? We will see how the—how the votes are cast. Neither of the—actually, one of them is a leading candidate.

So will Liberians welcome them? Let us see how the votes are cast. But I think it is a well-known fact in Liberia that several members of the Liberian Government and at least two candidates in the current elections have citizenship in other countries.

But the Alien Law, Chapter 22, says that doesn't exist and it is illegal.

Mr. DONOVAN. Mr. Nackerdien, was just wondering if you could tell us about how—again, talking about confidence, I think in your testimony it is about 54 percent of Liberian voters believe that the national elections back in 2011 were free and complete and fair, and I think in 2014, 3 years later, that was up to 78 percent.

What inspires this confidence? Mr. Peterson was telling me about the commission. What inspires this confidence that the Liberians have in the election process in such a short period of time that increased so dramatically?

Mr. NACKERDIEN. Thank you, Mr. Chairman.

I think the one thing that one could very specifically point to is running an election during a crisis. The 2014 elections happened during the Ebola crisis and the commission managed to very ably navigate a very complex time to manage that election and that is a direct testimony to how ordinary citizens respond to credible elections.

A process happening in the crisis I believe maneuvered—I think that could most clearly demonstrate where that change has come from.

Mr. DONOVAN. And my last question before I turn it over to the ranking member, Mr. Fomunyoh, there are many concerns about voter registration, timeliness.

We heard in the first panel about the rainy season now and the timeliness of the elections, and Dr. Curtis had noted that perhaps even the qualification of some of the candidates who hold American citizenship or citizenship from other countries may be a factor in when people are voting.

Do you anticipate that some of these issues are going to have a serious impact on the elections next month and what is your opinion on that?

Mr. FOMUNYOH. Having—Mr. Chairman, having just returned from Liberia as part of the pre-election assessment mission, the NDI delegation raised these issues with the Election Commission, with the political leaders as well as with representatives of Liberia and civil society organizations.

There was a sense that the registration period did allow for Liberians of voting age—eligible voters to register. There was a voter verification period during which the initial registry was made available so that citizens could verify that their names were properly recorded on the voter rolls and now the Election Commission is in the process of finalizing the voter registry.

The commission has promised to make that final voter registry available to political parties so that they will be able to verify in time.

I think we were told by September 15 that that final list will be available to political parties so they can begin the process of verifying to make sure that all of their supporters that are of voting age and that did participate in the voter registration process will be on the voter rolls.

Of course, with every election you cannot anticipate in advance the issues that will come up. But we will be looking very keenly to see if any Liberians that were of voting age and that were properly registered didn't find their names on the voter rolls or were disenfranchised because of any shortcomings on the part of the Election Commission or on the part of the poll workers.

Mr. DONOVAN. Thank you very much.

I yield to the ranking member, Ms. Bass.

Ms. BASS. Thank you very much, Mr. Chair.

I wanted to say a few things before asking questions and I wanted to begin with Mr. Peterson.

You cited in your comments—you ran through a number of countries that have had peaceful transfers of power, and I think it is important to note that because we often focus on those countries that don't have a peaceful transition.

And I think after the next year when all is said and done over all of the elections that have taken place over the continent, the vast majority are going to be a peaceful transfer of power and I think we need to keep that in mind.

I always think it is important in the United States that we begin to look at the continent of Africa differently and as opposed to a land of problems but a land of opportunities.

And I also want to mention in terms of Liberia because we keep making references to the connections between the United States and Liberia and I, first of all, feel that connection personally, considering that when the country of Liberia was established it was in conjunction with African American—enslaved African Americans and for all I know, some of my ancestors could have been on those boats going back to Liberia.

But since the average African American has no idea where their families come from or what happened to their families, to me there is a personal connection.

And I think as our country begins to reconcile with our history, we need to acknowledge that the Americans that went over to Liberia were enslaved African Americans.

So I wanted to first ask Dr. Curtis, because you mentioned DACA and you mentioned TPS, and I was wondering what is happening with the diaspora.

I do have to extend to you as well as to our presiding chairperson the opportunity to come next Friday to the Congressional Black Caucus Foundation African Brain Trust where Johnson Sirleaf will be there.

And we will make sure that you have that information because perhaps folks from Staten Island—it is not that far—might want to come and attend the event and see their President make some comments for the last time in the United States before she leaves

office, or one of the last times anyway. I am sure she will be at-
tending other events and I know there is one that takes place a few
days later.

But I wanted to know if you could talk about what is going on
amongst the diaspora community regarding DACA as well as TPS,
which did expire. So what does that mean? Microphone.

Ms. CURTIS. I am sorry. I will address DACA first. The disman-
tling of that protection for children is unfortunate, and as an edu-
cator who serviced a large immigrant community on Staten Island,
I understand the fear that now exists with families because it took
some convincing for us in the Liberian community and the education community to convince families that it is okay—you should
go ahead——

Ms. BASS. Right.

MS. CURTIS [continuing]. And apply for DACA.

Ms. BASS. Right.

Ms. CURTIS. Now, these families have outed themselves——

Ms. BASS. Right.

Ms. CURTIS [continuing]. And put themselves at extreme risk at
a time when that protection has been snatched away.

In the case of TPS, the United States of America has opened its
doors, as I said, to Liberians in a time of great need. And even as
Liberia has made great strides in reestablishing a democracy, there
are many reasons why families need to continue to live here in the
United States and TPS offered them that legal status. Having it
terminated on May 21st again put many families into hiding again.

Ms. BASS. Okay. What does that mean? Because since it expired, are
they subject to deportation? Can ICE pass by, since they are
also outed as well?

I mean, is there a list that ICE could essentially go pick everybody up whose TPS has expired?

Ms. CURTIS. I believe ICE has access to all of the information for
people who file for TPS, and if they decided that they wanted to
do a roundup that they could. I hope they don't.

But people who applied for TPS believed in a system that was
providing them legal status and that system now has terminated
that legal status. And so all of their—and these were all law-abiding citizens.

Criminals don't go and register with the government. These were
all—unless they are forced to—but these were all law-abiding citizens who were working in this country and now don't have that. And
I am not sure that the—that the systems in Liberia are prepared to absorb any mass migration back to Liberia.

Ms. BASS. Do you know what the numbers are?

Ms. CURTIS. I don't have the numbers off the top of my head. But
I will—I will research them and let Congress——

Ms. BASS. Between DACA and TPS I think it would be important
to know what the numbers are.

Ms. CURTIS. DACA, yes Congressman Donovan's office.

Ms. BASS. Thank you, and you should know that we are working
on it. So I am hopeful that we will come to a resolution around
DACA and I am hopeful that we will come to a resolution around
TPS.

My fear, though, is that how long that is going to take us. Sometimes it takes us a long time to act. But we can act quickly. We
can, and I am hopeful that we will.

Let me—I am sorry?

Ms. CURTIS. I will be reporting for you in that regard.

Ms. BASS. Yes. Absolutely.

But I wanted to talk now about or ask some questions of our
final—our next two panellists about the election and just a couple
of points.

One, I wanted to know, is the election just 1 day? As I mentioned, I participated as an observer in the election in Kenya, and
it was 1 day but it was a national holiday so everybody had the
day off and the polls were open from 6:00 to 5:00 in the evening.
And then in Kenya there was the full observer—observation mission.

So, you know, there was NDI. There was the AU, the EU, the
Carter Center, ECOWAS, and I am wondering if it will be a full-
blown observation mission as it was in Kenya. For either of you.

Mr. NACKERDIEN. Thank you, ma'am.

Yes, elections will be 1 day. Polls will be open on the 10th of October and I think people will be very interested to see how quickly
the election result actually comes back.

As far as we understand, and my colleague from NDI will talk
more about that, there are full-blown delegations from all the
major observer missions.

This is the—one of the top five elections that will be watched on
the African continent—following Kenya, Rwanda, and there are already groups from the Carter Center—long-term observer groups.

NDI has been there and the European Union has also been on
the ground working with domestic observer groups as well.

Ms. BASS. You know, and perhaps before you answer, you know,
Dr. Curtis raised the issue that one of the leading candidates—his
citizenship is questionable.

And I just wonder, especially given what happened in Kenya,
which was shocking to me, you know, with the Supreme Court, and
I am just wondering if this issue is a part of the campaign—when
you were there.

Mr. FOMUNYOH. When I was there, we—our delegation met with
all of the top candidates and the issue was not raised directly with
our delegation.

But we also were informed that in recent months the Election
Commission as well as the Supreme Court has made some rulings
that have been diversely interpreted by different segments of the
Liberian population and we make reference to that issue in the delegation statement.

If I could also answer on the delegations, that NDI will be field-
ing a full-blown delegation. We regret very much that you will not
be able to——

Ms. BASS. So do I.

Mr. FOMUNYOH [continuing]. Provide the leadership that you provided on the Kenya delegation.

Ms. BASS. Thank you.

Mr. FOMUNYOH. But we are going to take a second chance with
your schedule for November because——

Ms. BASS. Oh.

Mr. FOMUNYOH [continuing]. Of the very strong likelihood that there will a run-off election, given that there are 20 Presidential candidates and there is an estimation that none of the candidates would be able to obtain 50 percent plus one vote in the—in the first round.

Ms. BASS. Do they have the dates of the final or——

Mr. FOMUNYOH. They don't have the date yet but it is likely going to be at some point early November.

Ms. BASS. Okay.

Mr. FOMUNYOH. We will check with your staff, certainly.

Ms. BASS. Please.

Mr. FOMUNYOH. But we know that the Carter Center is going to field an international delegation. The European Union will send an international delegation as well as the African Union and the ECOWAS, which is the subregional entity for West African states.

Could I just add one last comment——

Ms. BASS. Sure.

Mr. FOMUNYOH [continuing]. With regards to your observation, Congresswoman Bass, on what has happened with political leadership in Africa in the past few years and to underscore the fact that when you look at West Africa, which is ECOWAS, that of the 15 countries that currently make up West Africa, 14 of them have had a renewal of political leadership through the ballot box in elections that have been accepted by the citizens of those countries as well as the international community as credible and free and fair.

And in those 14 countries, 14 of the 15 heads of states are serving their second term at the highest and none of them has exceeded the constitutional mandate that is required in most of those countries.

So when you look at the continent, West Africa has really made tremendous progress with regards to the ability of renewed political leadership through meaningful and credible elections.

Ms. BASS. Wonderful. Thank you very much.

And I don't know, Mr. Peterson, if you would like to have any concluding comments.

Mr. PETERSON. Well, I will just echo Chris' comments about West Africa. I think it really has become a bastion of democracy. That is not to underestimate the serious problems that they have—you know, corruption, the insecurity.

But I think that we in the United States would do well to pay a lot more attention to it. Democracy in many other parts of the world is under a lot of pressure. But I think we can be inspired by what is going on in West Africa.

Ms. BASS. But we need to pay attention to it, huh? Is that what you just said?

Thank you.

Mr. DONOVAN. Well, I thank all of the panellists for their insight, their experience, and sharing their thoughts with us and I thank my friend from California, Ms. Bass, for her participation, and Chairman Royce and Chairman Smith.

Without objection, all witnesses' full statements will be entered into the record of this hearing, and this hearing is now adjourned.

[Whereupon, at 4:01 p.m., the committee was adjourned.]

APPENDIX

SUBCOMMITTEE HEARING NOTICE
COMMITTEE ON FOREIGN AFFAIRS
U.S. HOUSE OF REPRESENTATIVES
WASHINGTON, DC 20515-6128

Subcommittee on Africa, Global Health, Global Human Rights, and International Organizations
Christopher H. Smith (R-NJ), Chairman

September 12, 2017

TO: MEMBERS OF THE COMMITTEE ON FOREIGN AFFAIRS

You are respectfully requested to attend an OPEN hearing of the Committee on Foreign Affairs, to be held by the Subcommittee Africa, Global Health, Global Human Rights, and International Organizations in Room 2172 of the Rayburn House Office Building (and available live on the Committee website at http://www.ForeignAffairs.house.gov):

DATE: Wednesday, September 13, 2017

TIME: 2:00 p.m.

SUBJECT: The Future of Democracy and Governance in Liberia

WITNESSES: Panel I
                     The Honorable Donald Yamamoto
                     Acting Assistant Secretary
                     Bureau of African Affairs
                     U.S. Department of State

                     Ms. Cheryl Anderson
                     Acting Assistant Administrator
                     Bureau for Africa
                     U.S. Agency for International Development

                     Panel II
                     Mr. Dave Peterson
                     Senior Director
                     Africa Programs
                     National Endowment for Democracy

                     Ms. Aurelia Curtis
                     Founder and Executive Director
                     Weeks Educational and Social Advocacy Project

                     Mr. Rushdi Nackerdien
                     Regional Director for Africa
                     International Foundation for Electoral Systems

                     Christopher Fomunyoh, Ph.D.
                     Senior Associate and Regional Director for Central and West Africa
                     National Democratic Institute

By Direction of the Chairman

COMMITTEE ON FOREIGN AFFAIRS

MINUTES OF SUBCOMMITTEE ON *Africa, Global Health, Global Human Rights, and International Organizations* HEARING

Day_*Wednesday*_ Date_____*9/13/17*_____ Room_____*2172*_____

Starting Time ___*2:08pm*___ Ending Time ___*4:00pm*___

Recesses |__*1*__| (*2:53pm* to *2:56pm*) (____to ____) (____to ____) (____to ____) (____to ____) (____to ____)

Presiding Member(s)

Chris Smith/Daniel Donovan

Check all of the following that apply:

Open Session ☑
Executive (closed) Session ☐
Televised ☐

Electronically Recorded (taped) ☐
Stenographic Record ☑

TITLE OF HEARING:

The Future of Democracy and Governance in Liberia

SUBCOMMITTEE MEMBERS PRESENT:

Smith, Bass, Donovan

NON-SUBCOMMITTEE MEMBERS PRESENT: *(Mark with an * if they are not members of full committee.)*

Royce

HEARING WITNESSES: Same as meeting notice attached? Yes ☑ No ☐
(If "no", please list below and include title, agency, department, or organization.)

STATEMENTS FOR THE RECORD: *(List any statements submitted for the record.)*

TIME SCHEDULED TO RECONVENE _________
or
TIME ADJOURNED ___*4:00pm*___

Subcommittee Staff Associate

www.ingramcontent.com/pod-product-compliance
Lightning Source LLC
Chambersburg PA
CBHW080857260726
48660CB00009B/3343